A ROMAN FRONTIER FORT IN SCOTLAND
ELGINHAUGH

A ROMAN FRONTIER FORT IN SCOTLAND
ELGINHAUGH

WILLIAM S. HANSON

TEMPUS

First published 2007

Tempus Publishing
Cirencester Road, Chalford,
Stroud, Gloucestershire, GL6 8PE
www.tempus-publishing.com

Tempus Publishing is an imprint of NPI Media Group

British Library Cataloguing in Publication Data.
A catalogue record for this book is available from the British Library.

ISBN 978 0 7524 4113 9

Typesetting and origination by NPI Media Group
Printed in Great Britain

CONTENTS

ACKNOWLEDGEMENTS

An excavation project as large as that discussed here is very much a matter of teamwork, particularly in the field. I am much indebted to the many individuals, too numerous to name, who laboured for many weeks in the field over the two seasons of the excavation, for their contribution to its success. The post-excavation process is no less the product of teamwork. Particular thanks must go to Peter Yeoman and John Terry, both of whom worked on the site as assistant director and site supervisor respectively, who undertook the integration of all the site records and the preliminary stratigraphic assessment; and to Keith Speller, who masterminded both the photography and the planning process on site and subsequently produced all the plans and section drawings. Other drawings should be credited as follows: Yvonne Beadnell (*60*); John Dore (*56, 59*); Dennis Gallacher (*63*); John Gater (*4*); Elizabeth Lazenby (*32, 45-7, 50-1, 54, 62, 68-9*); Lorraine McEwan (*6, 12*); Ioana Oltean (*7* based on data provided by Beccy Jones); Patricia Roberts (*55, 57*); and Jill Sievewright (*48-9*). I am grateful to the Royal Commission on the Ancient and Historical Monuments of Scotland for permission to reproduce figures *1* and *2* and to the Hunterian Museum and Art Gallery for permission to reproduce figures *11* and *42* and *colour plate 5*.

Some 23 specialists examined and reported on the various categories of finds from the site, some dealing with large quantities of material, others only a few finds. To them all I wish to record my heartfelt gratitude for their assistance and ready co-operation. This book has drawn particularly on the detailed reports by Lindsay Allason-Jones on the small objects, Donal Bateson on the coins, Alan Clapham on the plant remains, Anne Crone on the waterlogged wood, the late Camilla Dickson on the pollen analysis, John Dore on the coarseware, Willy Groenman-van Waateringe on the leather, the late Brian Hartley on the samian ware, Kay Hartley on the mortaria, David Jordan on the soils and sediments, Euan MacKie on the rotary quernstones, Jenny Price and Sally Worrell on the glass, Liz Slater on the metallurgical analysis and Catherine Smith on the animal bones. Material from Gordon Maxwell's report on the bathhouse has also been incorporated. Thanks must go to Historic Scotland who funded the excavation and invited me to direct the work; and to Glasgow University for releasing me from my normal duties both for the period of the excavation and for the early stages of the preparation of the full excavation report, as well as for continuing to provide support during its too lengthy gestation. Finally, my thanks to David Breeze, who kindly read and commented on the text.

LIST OF ILLUSTRATIONS
AND TABLES

COLOUR PLATES

TABLES

ONE

DISCOVERY AND EXCAVATION

DISCOVERY

The Roman fort at Elginhaugh near Dalkeith in the Lothian Region was discovered in the dry summer of 1979 during aerial reconnaissance by the Royal Commission on the Ancient and Historical Monuments of Scotland. I was sitting in the rear of the aircraft at the time, alongside Gordon Maxwell who was directing the survey programme, in order to gain more experience of aerial work with a view to undertaking my own aerial survey in the western lowlands of Scotland. I saw and photographed the parchmarks in the grass below (*colour plate 1*), and recognised that they probably represented the line of Dere Street, the main Roman road running north into Scotland up the eastern side of the country. What I did not appreciate at the time was the full significance of the apparent T-junction in the road. This suggested to Gordon that there must be some form of site there, and almost certainly that of a Roman fort. Little did I imagine that several years later I would spend almost a year working in the field below us on the excavation of that site.

Gordon Maxwell, keeping his suspicions to himself for the time being, arranged several months later in December 1979 to visit the site and undertake some small-scale trial trenching to check his hypothesis. A few judiciously placed trenches confirmed the survival of a clay rampart, metalled roads (which had created the parchmarks), ovens and the construction trenches of timber buildings. Only one phase of Roman occupation was indicated, dated by pottery finds to the late first century AD, but he also found some pre-Roman Iron Age pottery, in what he interpreted as a construction trench for a timber structure, hinting at the presence of a native settlement beneath the fort (see chapter seven).

The contribution of aerial reconnaissance to our understanding of the archaeology of the Scottish Lowlands in all periods from the Neolithic onwards is considerable, serving to offset to a large extent the relatively low level of archaeological visibility of extant remains in the zone where centuries of ploughing have largely destroyed all visible traces of earlier sites. Though often insufficiently appreciated, it is no exaggeration to claim that aerial reconnaissance has made the single most important contribution to our improved appreciation of the density, diversity and widespread distribution of archaeological sites in recent decades. Something of the order of 50 per cent of all the sites currently known in the lowland arable zone have been found from the air, particularly through the medium of cropmarks. It is through aerial reconnaissance that we have come to recognise that these lowland fertile zones have always been, as they remain today, the core areas for settlement in Scotland.

The contribution of air reconnaissance lies in the first instance in the discovery of new sites, which continues each year, though with varying levels of intensity according to fluctuating weather patterns, and the continued enhancement of our knowledge of known sites. Its impact on the understanding of the Roman period has been particularly strong, partly because early practitioners of the art in Scotland, such as Professor J.K.S. St Joseph and Gordon Maxwell, had research interests strongly focused in the Roman period, and partly because the morphological characteristics of Roman military sites are such as to make them more readily identifiable. Our understanding of Roman campaigns in Scotland is based to a large extent on the distribution and morphology of Roman temporary camps, the vast majority of which are aerial photographic discoveries (7). Apart from Elginhaugh itself, large numbers of Roman forts in Scotland, such as Glenlochar, Easter Happrew, Dalswinton, Drumlanrig, Barochan, Mollins, Drumquhassle, Doune, Malling, Cargill, Inverquharity and Stracathro owe their discovery to aerial reconnaissance. Though the existence of the site has been known since the sixteenth century, our confidence in the accuracy of the complete plan of the legionary fortress at Inchtuthil owes as much to the excellence of the aerial photographic coverage as to the relatively limited excavation of the interior, with the former informing the conducting of the latter.

Thus, once identified, the fort site at Elginhaugh was re-photographed by the RCAHMS over several years, providing additional information about the nature and extent of the remains. Unusually, the fort was defined from the air entirely by the roads within it, rather than by positive cropmarks of its surrounding ditches, though a number of ditches visible towards the north-western limit of the field did indicate the presence of a probable annexe (1). This repeated aerial reconnaissance also revealed the outline of the stone walls of a bathhouse in July 1984, showing as a parchmark in the grass in the next field to the south by the river (2), which Gordon Maxwell also confirmed by trial excavation in the early winter of that year (see chapter six).

Location

The fort is situated on the flat crest of a steep scarp overlooking the river North Esk some 2.5km (1.5 miles) south-west of its confluence with the South Esk (3). That the crossing of the river would have been of interest to the Romans had already been indicated on the basis of aerial survey and excavation several years earlier when parts of two of the three Roman temporary camps at Eskbank on the other side of the river were excavated ahead of housing development. The fort had been preserved in a small triangle of semi-permanent pasture edged by plantation and bounded to the north-west by a modern road, to the north-east by a long dismantled railway line and to the south by a combination of road and river. Very little survived on the surface, though traces of

1 Aerial photograph of the fort at Elginhaugh in 1984 showing the main Roman road, intervallum road and annexe ditches. *Crown copyright: Royal Commission on the Ancient and Historical Monuments of Scotland*

a subrectangular platform defined by the levelled fort rampart were faintly visible to the discerning eye. All other surface remains had been removed by ploughing over a lengthy period. The site had been under pasture for some years, but before that, still within living memory, had been a market garden. The subsoil consists of banded sands and silty clay with, as a result, considerable differential drainage and a perched water table.

The fort straddles what was at the time of its discovery the most northerly identified stretch of Dere Street. This Roman road ran north from York via the important base at Newstead in Tweeddale. Beyond Elginhaugh, Dere Street seems to be heading north-west following the line of the modern A7 before turning sharply northwards pointing towards Edinburgh Castle Rock. It would then presumably have turned west via Gogar, where temporary camps have been identified, and Ingliston, where a Roman milestone has been recorded, towards the fort at Camelon and the crossing of the Carron.

2 Aerial photograph showing the parchmarks of the stone walls of the bathhouse. *Crown copyright: Royal Commission on the Ancient and Historical Monuments of Scotland*

There can be little doubt that the fort at Elginhaugh was located to guard a river crossing, either by bridge or ford, since the North Esk is fordable in the immediate vicinity. The close juxtaposition of the fort and the crossing of that river by three modern arterial routes, the A68, the A7 and the now dismantled railway line, emphasise the strategic importance of this bridgehead position.

EXCAVATION STRATEGY AND TACTICS

The field in which the fort lay was purchased for development by the Scottish Development Agency (SDA) in 1985. In light of the aerial photographic discoveries made some years earlier, Historic Scotland (then known as Historic Buildings and Monuments, Scottish Development Department) decided that excavation was necessary, arranged for funding and invited me, as a specialist in Roman military timber buildings, to direct the project. The University of Glasgow, my employers then as now, were kind enough to appreciate the mutual benefits of allowing me time from my normal duties to undertake the work, and accordingly I was seconded to Historic Scotland for two years. After the excavation had been completed, the site was bought by the Scottish Widows Fund and Life Assurance Society who constructed their computer data centre there, located primarily over the site of the fort. The computer facility is now owned by the Royal Bank of Scotland and it is ironic that security at the site, in terms of local access, is now probably stronger than when it was a Roman fort. At the time of the excavation, however, the exact location and extent of the proposed development was unknown, so that potentially the whole 4.8ha (12 acres) field was under threat. Accordingly, Historic Scotland wished to examine as much of the field as was possible within the constraints of time and resources and together David Breeze, as the Inspector of Ancient Monuments with responsibility for Roman archaeology, and I identified five priorities to be addressed by the excavation: to recover the full plan and chronological development of the fort; to recover the full plan and chronological development of the postulated Iron Age settlement beneath it; to establish the plan and character of the features outside the fort, particularly in the annexe; to establish the nature of and potential Roman impact on the local environment and, finally, to determine as much as possible about the post-Roman use of the site.

Given the size and importance of the project, one of the largest single excavations funded by Historic Scotland up to that date, these proposals were published in *Scottish Archaeological Review* to promote discussion and feedback prior to the work commencing (though, in the event, none was forthcoming!). Since it was recognised that total stratigraphic excavation of such a large area in the time originally available (seven months) was not really feasible, the methodology proposed and subsequently employed was to strip the area by machine in order to recover basic plan information and then excavate selectively in order to test relationships, recover dateable material and take environmental samples. This was an exciting prospect, for it would be the first time that the complete layout of a timber-built auxiliary fort was going to be completely uncovered under modern, controlled archaeological conditions and the first time that any extensive area of a fort annexe was to be similarly investigated. Recognising that such a strategy might pose an additional threat to any remains of post-Roman use of the site, the field was shallow-ploughed and harrowed to facilitate fieldwalking to try to recover at least some artefactual remains in the ploughsoil before it was machined away, though in the event nothing of post-Roman significance was recovered apart from a few sherds of medieval pottery.

Machine stripping of the site began on 1 April 1986, a less than auspicious date as it turned out. To avoid the inconvenience and expense of removing topsoil from the field only to return it later, I decided to undertake the excavation in three stages. The obvious place to start was the site of the fort itself, so that some familiarity with the form and state of preservation of the archaeological remains might be gained where buildings were known to exist and their character was to some extent predictable, before turning to the less well understood areas within the annexe and outside the fort to the north. A limited

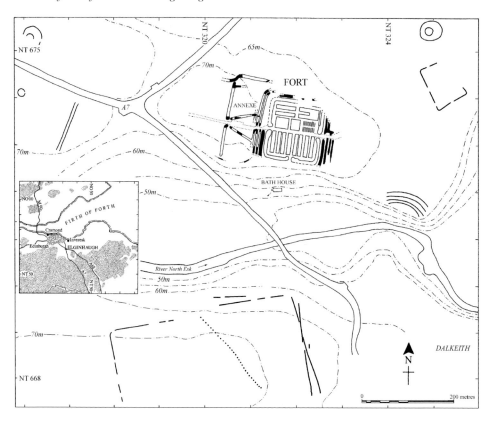

3 Elginhaugh, Midlothian: location plan of the fort and other sites attested by aerial photography in the immediate vicinity

area to the east of the fort was included in the first stage for purely logistical reasons, as access would have been difficult once the fort area had been stripped. Stage two was to have been the examination of the annexe to the west of the fort and stage three, the lowest priority, the area to the north where the ground began to slope away towards the entrance to the field and where nothing was visible on any of the aerial photographs.

In the event, neither time nor finances allowed complete stripping of the 4.8ha (12 acres) field. Two major problems were encountered which resulted in serious delays, a considerable increase in expenditure and not a few sleepless nights for me. The combination of high rainfall in April and May 1986 and the poorly draining silty clay soils across substantial parts of the fort site meant that machining was slower and subject to more delays than was anticipated. In addition, after the topsoil had been stripped, the upper soil horizon proved to be very heavily worm sorted because the addition of lime, which accompanies traditional market gardening, combined with occasional cultivation, long-term pasture and the aeration of the upper parts of the soil, had resulted in a large worm population. Constant mixing and remixing of the soil by worms over many decades, combined with disturbance caused by the penetration of tap-roots, had the effect of masking the changes of texture and colour which normally facilitate the recognition of disturbance of the soil by human agencies. Thus, the anticipated negative archaeological features, pits and construction trenches, were virtually invisible despite careful cleaning, which revealed only the roads and surviving drains (*colour plate 2*). Even when limited areas within the fort were taken down further by hand in shallow spits, for example across what subsequently was identified as the officers' quarters of barrack 5 in the south-east corner of the fort, the construction trenches of the timber buildings remained stubbornly undetectable.

The one exception was in the north-west corner of the fort where ploughing had already removed the worm-sorted horizon, including all road surfaces and even drains, revealing the central sector of two barracks (nos 1 and 2) (*colour plate 3*). Accordingly, I decided that the only way that the rest of the fort plan was going to become visible was to take fairly drastic action and remove a further 20-40cm by machine across the rest of the area of the fort, working out from these visible traces, even though this would involve removing some archaeological layers. This decision was not taken lightly, but there was no alternative if anything was to be achieved within the available timescale. This secondary machining also added considerably both to the costs of the excavation and to the time taken to establish the plan of the fort, so that in 1986 the excavation did not progress beyond stage 1 before time ran out and the available budget was spent.

Appreciating the academic importance of some examination of the annexe, additional funds were made available by Historic Scotland in 1987 and further access to the site was kindly allowed by SDA, enabling excavation to recommence in June 1987 for a further two months. Both the additional limited funds and the restricted timescale required a different strategy to be adopted from that which had originally been envisaged. This involved more selective excavation within the annexe, based on information from the aerial photographs (see *1*) and specially commissioned magnetometer survey (*4*). Key points around the defensive perimeter of the annexe were targeted, while examination of the interior focused on the area adjacent to the line of the road from the west gate of the fort. Large trenches were laid out and the topsoil removed by machine. Even with this more restricted approach in the second season, by the end of 1987 a total of some 2.4ha (6 acres) of the field had been examined by excavation, making Elginhaugh one of the largest rescue excavation projects ever undertaken in Scotland.

Finally, in February and March 1989 a watching brief was undertaken by John Terry, who had worked on the site as an area supervisor in both 1986 and 1987, in the adjacent field to the south of the fort during the installation of drainage pipes for the ongoing development. The opportunity was also taken at this time to dig by hand two small trenches to address specific questions about the southern perimeter and internal subdivision of the annexe.

INNOVATIVE RECORDING METHODS

Recognising that the time scale for the excavation of such a large area was always likely to be tight, I was determined that the most advanced recording techniques would be

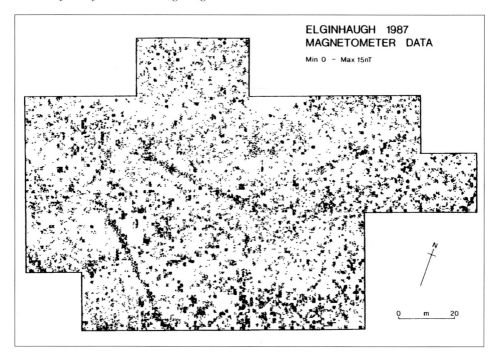

ELGINHAUGH 1987
MAGNETOMETER DATA

Min 0 – Max 15nT

4 Dot density plot of magnetic anomalies in the central area of the annexe

applied, most of which are still not standard practice even today, in order to streamline the process as much as possible. In particular, this involved on-site computer recording of contexts and finds, including their three-dimensional location established by Electronic Distance Measurer (EDM), using a system developed by Dominic Powlesland at Heslerton in Yorkshire. All primary context records were created by direct input on site into small hand-held computers issued to each site supervisor, though not all them were entirely happy with this arrangement and most preferred their green, hardback notebooks, carried with them at all times as if they were some badge of office. The hand-held computers were the forerunners of today's palmtop computers, though much less powerful, and were loaded with a simple database form designed for coded entries and some minimal text field description. They were regularly downloaded onto floppy disk on site, utilising what was laughingly referred to as a 'portable' computer, but which was distinctly heavy and unwieldy by today's standards, and printed out for pasting into the supervisors' green notebooks, one context on each page, for ease of subsequent reference, annotation, editing and amendment. All primary finds records, including preliminary identifications, were similarly created as the finds went through standard processing procedures, involving basic cleaning and identification. The three-dimensional location of all finds and contexts was determined by EDM and separately recorded on site, also on a hand-held computer. At an early stage of the post-excavation process, the various floppy disks, including those containing locational information from the EDM, were amalgamated into a single integrated database of finds and contexts that facilitated sorting across any of the basic data fields. Though the site plans were generated by hand in the normal way, they were digitised at an early stage of the post-excavation process to facilitate the easy production of plans at any scale and to allow their integration with computer-generated artefact distributions using Dominic Powlesland's own geographical information system (GIS) software. This provided a powerful analytical tool, though its potential was not exploited as much as it might have been, largely as a result of my own comparatively limited IT skills, but the database remains available for further manipulation in the future. This type of computerised approach to post-excavation data handling and graphics is more readily achieved today, particularly with the much faster machines now available. To put this into perspective, in 1987 it would take over forty-five minutes to load the overall site plan and display it on screen; the same plan today would appear in seconds.

Though standard photography was used on site, video recording was employed as an integral part of the photographic record. During the course of the excavation, high quality analogue format video (low band U-matic) was used to replace much of the standard black and white photographic record. In addition to any set-piece shots of areas or features taken before and after excavation, making full use of the facility to pan round to contextualise features or zoom in to note detail, any on-going work was also recorded, usually on a twice-daily basis, to produce what was in effect a video diary of the excavation with built-in commentary. As a result, a total of over twenty-four hours of video footage was recorded. This primary record proved to be of immense value during the preliminary stages of post-excavation analysis, allowing many of the various questions and uncertainties about contextual relationships, which always arise after the excavation has been completed, to be checked or reviewed. Moreover, as with the computerised database, it provides a uniquely detailed archive of the progress of the excavation.

Despite these various innovations, publication of the full site report has been too long delayed, though a brief glossy, full-colour interim account was published by Peter Yeoman (who had acted as assistant director during both seasons of excavation) and myself, entitled *Elginhaugh: a Roman fort and its environs*, with the aid of a 'Glenfiddich Living Scotland Award' award in 1988. The full excavation report, which is currently in press, is in excess of 235,000 words in length and contains contributions from some twenty-seven specialists commenting on the artefactual and ecofactual material or structural evidence. It is inevitable that such an endeavour will take time to co-ordinate, but the bulk of the report was complete more than a decade ago. The subsequent delay was the result of work pressure on certain specialists who are in heavy demand for their expertise, acquired over many years of detailed study. When the final specialist reports were submitted, I had to revise and update the text before it could finally be submitted for publication, though this did give me the opportunity to completely rewrite the interpretation of the likely garrison in light of new work in northern Britain and Germany (see chapter four). What follows here is a presentation of the main results of the excavation within their wider context.

TWO

THE FLAVIAN FRONTIER

HISTORICAL BACKGROUND

After the major setback of the Boudican rebellion in the reign of Nero in AD 60, Roman conquest and concomitant expansion was not resumed in Britain until in AD 71 under a new imperial house, the Flavians. T. Flavius Vespasianus (Vespasian), who became emperor in AD 69 after triumphing in a brief civil war, was a man of considerable military experience; he had even served in Britain, commanding one of the legions at the time of the invasion in AD 43. Where better to pursue imperialist ambitions and re-assert Roman power, whose perception had been tarnished by the civil war. The advance progressed rapidly over the next fifteen years under successive governors, during which time military occupation was extended north and west across northern England, Wales and Scotland. Conquest of much of this area is generally attributed to Gaius Julius Agricola, governor of the province from AD 77-83, about whose activities we are particularly well informed because he had the historical good sense to see his daughter marry a young senator and aspiring historian, Cornelius Tacitus. Tacitus's *Agricola*, a laudatory biography of his father-in-law, has survived and provides the narrative framework against which the archaeological evidence for this period has traditionally been set.

According to Tacitus, the conquest of Scotland began with Agricola's third campaign in AD 79, which extended as far north as the estuary of the river Tay, apparently meeting little resistance despite the depth of penetration into new territory. Thereafter it seems to have been something of a stop-go affair as emperors and, with them, policy changed twice in four years; the death of Vespasian in AD 79 was followed by that of his successor, his son Titus, in AD 81. Agricola's fourth and fifth seasons seem to have been spent consolidating what had been gained. This involved the establishment of close military control across Lowland Scotland, manifested in the form of a network of forts and fortlets at regular intervals of 16-20 miles, usually referred to as a day's march apart, linked by a road system (5). It is evident from the distribution as currently understood that a number of Flavian forts in Lowland Scotland remain undiscovered, particularly in the south-west, where no installations are known to the west of Gatehouse-of-Fleet. Nonetheless, the general pattern is sufficiently clear, with forts controlling the main routeways and river crossings. This period of consolidation is the strategic context for the placing of a garrison at Elginhaugh, which is the most northerly Flavian fort known on Dere Street, the main north–south communication route on the eastern side of the country. It may also mark the junction with a cross route approaching from the south-west, though its line is not known beyond Silverburn just south of Penicuik. The fort at Elginhaugh was clearly sited to control a river crossing. Indeed, its strategic location within the Roman road network, underlined by the nearby convergence of two modern major roads, was evident before the excavation began.

According to Tacitus, who is unusually geographically specific at this point in his narrative, this consolidation process also involved the construction of a relatively short-lived frontier across the Forth-Clyde isthmus:

> If the valour of our army and the glory of Rome had permitted such a thing, a good place for halting the advance was found in Britain itself. The Forth and Clyde, carried inland for a great distance by the tides of opposite seas, are separated by only a narrow neck of land. This isthmus was now firmly held by garrisons. (*Agricola 23*)

This temporary halt seems to have coincided with the brief reign of the Emperor Titus, Vespasian's elder son, who died in September AD 81, and seems to reflect a deliberate policy on his part not to continue with further expansion. The fort at Elginhaugh would have been linked to this frontier by road, though the line is not known in any detail. It may have followed an inland route via Gogar and Linlithgow to the fort at Camelon, which was an important gathering ground for troops heading north and marked the point at which the only Roman road to the north crossed the river Forth at the furthest limit of its navigability from the sea. The physical remains of this line of fortifications are still not well attested, but other installations include the fort at Barochan beyond the Clyde and the small fort at Mollins (*colour plate 4*), both discovered from the air. Other sites have been postulated beneath some of the later Antonine Wall forts, though the evidence is limited to a small number of Flavian coins and a few fragment of pottery or glass rather than any structural evidence, so the identifications should be treated with some caution (see below).

This temporary frontier may also have followed the Roman road beyond the isthmus as far as Bertha on the river Tay. Along this line a series of forts, fortlets, and timber watchtowers have been discovered, particularly along the Gask Ridge. This system has all the hallmarks of a frontier, with spacing between forts reduced to half a day's march or less, interspersed fortlets and a closer watch provided by the construction of watchtowers at intervals of 800-1500m (*6*). There is still considerable disagreement about the precise date and context of this system, but a link with Agricola's halt on the Forth–Clyde isthmus in his fourth campaign seems at present the best explanation and would make this the earliest artificially defined frontier in the Roman Empire.

The general historical summary presented above has been challenged in recent years. In particular there has been increasing debate concerning the extent to which Tacitus' surviving account of the military achievements of Agricola's governorship is biased and exaggerated. Certainly there has been an unfortunate tendency amongst Roman

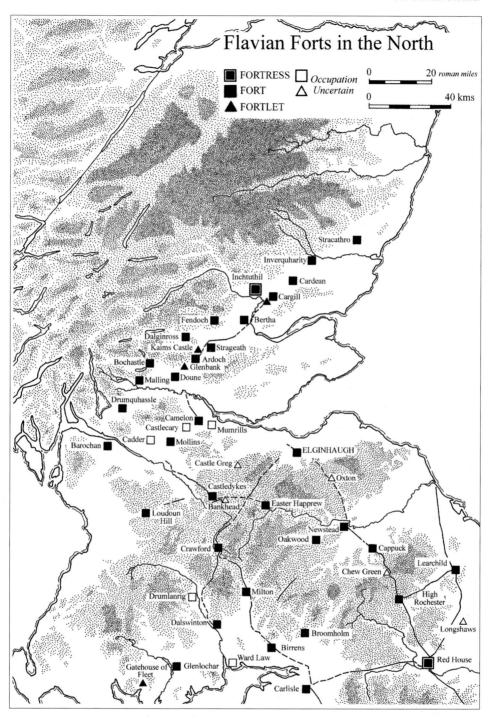

5 Distribution map of Flavian forts in north Britain

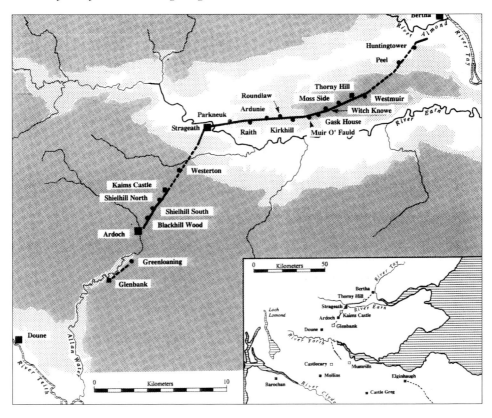

6 The Gask 'frontier'

military archaeologists to assume that the sites they excavated were Agricolan on no stronger evidence than that account, leading to a somewhat circular argument whereby the same sites were then used to support the accuracy of the literary evidence. Careful consideration of other literary sources and some independently dated archaeological material led to increasing speculation, not least by the current author, that one of Agricola's two immediate predecessors as governor, Petillius Cerialis (AD 71-73/4), was actually responsible for the conquest of northern England and may even have penetrated north of the Tyne–Solway isthmus. The subsequent acquisition of dendrochronological dates of AD 72 for the felling of timbers used in the construction of the auxiliary fort at Carlisle, which had been preserved by subsequent waterlogging of the site, has confirmed that that fort was indeed established as a result of Cerialis' campaign against the Brigantes. This, in conjunction with the identification of another early Flavian fort in Cumbria at Blennerhasset, has in recent years fuelled additional speculation about the origins of the forts in Lowland Scotland and, indeed, those even further north beyond the Forth-Clyde isthmus.

The basis for this speculation has been twofold. Firstly, the recognition of occasional pieces of pottery and glass of typologically pre- or early Flavian date, and of similarly dated coins, from several fort sites in Lowland Scotland, such as Newstead and particularly Camelon, as well as from forts beyond the Forth–Clyde line, such as Strageath and Cardean. Secondly, the hints of more than one phase of occupation at a number of the latter sites, including some of the watchtowers on the Gask Ridge. The argument then follows that the sites must have been occupied for longer than previously assumed if they show more than one phase and, since the date of abandonment of the more northerly forts is fixed to immediately after AD 86 on the basis of the latest dated coins recovered (see below), their occupation must have begun earlier than previously supposed, as hinted at by the early Flavian finds.

There are, however a number of difficulties with this model. There is considerable danger in taking a limited number of 'early' finds, such as sherds of pottery or glass, from an assemblage out of their wider context and using them to argue for an earlier foundation date for the site, as has been done recently in relation to several Flavian forts in Scotland. The garrison would not have been newly equipped with freshly manufactured material on its arrival at a new posting, but would have carried with it pottery and glass acquired over the previous decade or so, as has been attested for example by the presence of ceramic material from south-western England which seems to have accompanied the troops engaged in the early Flavian advance into Scotland. That any assemblage of material recovered from a site should, therefore, contain a few vessels which were already 'old' when eventually disposed of need occasion no surprise. Furthermore, as some of the mortaria produced locally at Elginhaugh serve to demonstrate, some typological forms continued to be manufactured after their main period of production was over. The same applies to some of the so-called pre-Flavian fine wares, such as Lyon ware, for which there is increasing evidence of manufacture and distribution continuing into the mid-Flavian period. The dating significance of any such finds must, therefore, be judged against the overall pattern of material from the site, not taken in isolation.

Similarly, differentiating between repairs, minor structural amendments and substantive changes representing different phases or periods of occupation can be difficult without relatively large-scale excavation. But even where such changes are attested, they can occur in a relatively short period of time and may have nothing other than local significance, as the evidence particularly from Elginhaugh indicates, where we see amendments to several of the barrack blocks and substantive changes of use in the annexe within less than a decade of occupation (see chapters four and five).

Finally, it is one thing to challenge the account provided by Tacitus in his *Agricola* in terms of its emphasis and bias. It has long been accepted that the work is not a simple historical narrative, but both a laudatory biography intended to portray Agricola in the best possible light and something of a political *apologia* for Tacitus himself. It is, however, entirely another thing to suggest, as David Woolliscroft and Birgitta Hoffman appear to do, that the whole basis of what was a near-contemporary record of events (it was published in *c.*AD 98 only fifteen to twenty years after the events it describes) is complete fabrication. So, though Petillius Cerialis may well have campaigned in Lowland Scotland, perhaps even founding one or two forts in the south-west beyond Carlisle, it is unlikely that he was responsible for the consolidation of the rest of Lowland Scotland and certainly not for any of the forts beyond the Forth-Clyde isthmus.

Indeed, Agricola may have been responsible for the abandonment of some forts established by Cerialis. The number of Flavian auxiliary forts currently known in north Britain already exceeds by over 50 per cent the number of units attested in the army of the province at the time, as understood from epigraphic and historical sources, and it is clear, on grounds of topography and logical strategic dispositions, that many more forts remain to be discovered. While it is possible that the size of the army was considerably larger than the sources attest, it is improbable that the figure is more than 100 per cent inaccurate. It seems likely, therefore, that Flavian forts in Wales and northern England may have been abandoned, either permanently or temporarily, in order to release the manpower to pursue the conquest of Scotland, as suggested at Hayton in Yorkshire or Caernarvon in north Wales.

According to Tacitus, Roman campaigning under Agricola was subsequently resumed, in the sixth and seventh year of his governorship (AD 82-3), probably as the result of the accession of Domitian as the new emperor in September AD 81. Complete conquest of the island was clearly the intention and campaigns were extended by both land and sea. The route taken skirting the Highlands up the east coast of Scotland is attested by series of 'marching' camps, the temporary accommodation of the troops on campaign, whose ditched outlines survive mainly only as cropmarks visible from the air (7). These temporary camps are notoriously difficult to date, but recent extensive rescue excavations at Kintore in Aberdeenshire revealed that the 110-acre camp, one of a series of similar size and shape, seems to have been occupied in both the first and third centuries, while further south in Fife a camp of similar size but different shape at Carey (Abernethy) produced Flavian pottery from a small-scale excavation across its ditch. Several smaller camps of up to 34 acres in area are also attested, some likely to be Flavian in date because of their distinctive 'Stracathro' gateway form. They do not, however, make a coherent group which can be related to any particular campaign and merely serve to emphasise the complexity of this phase of military activity.

Agricola's campaigns culminated in AD 83 in the battle of Mons Graupius, somewhere in north-east Scotland, at which the final resistance of the Caledonians was crushed. Much ink has been, and continues to be, spilt in debating where the battle took place. Most commentators assume a northerly location, since that is implied by the narrative of Tacitus, though the etymological link between the Grampian Mountains and Mons Graupius is the reverse of what one might expect. An error by an early editor of Tacitus' text produced Grampius instead of Graupius, and it is from this that the mountains, formerly known as 'the Mounth', subsequently acquired the name Grampians. None of the various sites which have been proposed are entirely convincing, though it remains possible that an accidental discovery of a mass burial of men and horses or substantial scatters of Roman weaponry may one day resolve the issue, as happened some years ago in Germany in identifying the site of the Varan disaster where the Romans lost three legions in the reign of Augustus. But taking the broad historical perspective, the precise location of the battle is unimportant. Only if it proved to be located considerably further north, such as in Caithness, or west, in the Highlands, would its discovery have any substantial impact on our interpretation of the character and extent of Agricola's

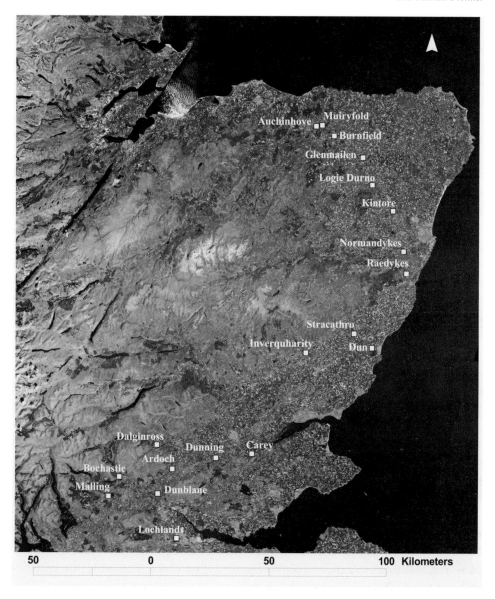

7 Distribution of Flavian temporary camps north of the Forth-Clyde isthmus plotted on a Landsat image

campaigns. However, the absence of place names in any of the Roman literary sources which might be located in the western mainland of Scotland makes the latter highly unlikely.

The battle was won with typical Roman efficiency, without even the necessity to deploy the legions, and was followed by a circumnavigation of the island by the Roman fleet. Further consolidation of the conquered area was then undertaken involving the construction of a number of forts. It has long been recognised that the density and spacing of Flavian military establishments north of the Forth-Clyde isthmus is likely to indicate a complex history of development (5). It has already been suggested above that the inner line of posts along the road from Camelon to Bertha were possibly the first to be built, perhaps as part of the consolidation of the isthmus under Agricola. Beyond that to the west, however, there is an outer line of forts skirting the Highlands, sometimes referred to as the 'glen-blocking forts', and a further line continuing north up Strathmore as far as Stracathro on the North Esk, the two lines pivoting on the legionary fortress at Inchtuthil just north of the Tay. That more than one phase of occupation was involved is strikingly indicated by the site at Cargill, where an auxiliary fort and large fortlet, both of Flavian date, are situated within 300m of each other. Other forts also provide hints of more than one phase of activity, though these may be no more than minor remodelling. At Strageath, a small granary was replaced by a probable stores building (though it was interpreted by the excavators as linked to the construction phase of the fort enclosure) and the interior of a barrack or stores building was partly rebuilt, while at Cardean, one barrack may have been replaced by a stores building. This pattern is reminiscent of the remodelling of some of the barrack interiors at Elginhaugh (see chapter four). Rather than necessarily indicating the longevity of occupation at these sites, however, it emphasises the fluidity of the situation shortly after successful military conquest.

Since such consolidation normally followed the successful subjugation of an area, all these sites are likely to have been constructed immediately after the Agricolan campaigns and probably, therefore, under the command of his unknown successor as governor. Archaeological support for this interpretation of events is provided by the fact that the legionary fortress at Inchtuthil, though probably already operative, was still in the course of construction on its abandonment in AD 87 or shortly thereafter. Work had yet to commence on the *praetorium*, the legionary legate's accommodation, on several of the senior officers' houses, at least two granaries and the main bath building, while the headquarters building is clearly too small for a legionary base and does not fully occupy the plot within which it is set, as if assembled rapidly as an interim measure. Finally, a small external bathhouse, probably intended for the officers, seems not to have been used, for the two stokeholes provided to heat the hot rooms had never been fired. Though there is inevitably some debate about how long it might have taken to build a turf and timber legionary fortress, figures of less than two years with a work-force of 1435 men or almost three years with a work force of 860 men have recently been argued by Elizabeth Shirley based on a very detailed assessment of the nature of the work and the resources required. Even allowing for those fairly wide parameters, it would seem therefore that the work is unlikely to have commenced before AD 85, or 84 at the earliest.

The intended function of these forts, particularly those in the Highland line, has again been much debated. Apart from their obvious role in consolidating the control of territory overrun, their location at the mouths of the glens clearly indicates that they were intended to control movement. Though the individual glens whose exits they marked were themselves of minor importance and not densely inhabited, they linked back into wider routeways through the Highlands both to the north and to the south. What is less clear is whether access to these routes was related to a further offensive into, or a defensive measure against opposition emanating out of, the Highland massif. However, the presence of a legionary fortress almost at the very limit of the occupied area smacks of the intention to continue the advance and push yet further, since once conquest was complete, legionary forces tended to be held in reserve not placed on the front line. Whether or not any such campaigns were undertaken is not known. Tacitus is silent on the matter, since the main protagonist of his story, Agricola, had been recalled to Rome at the end of an already lengthy term of office as governor in AD 83, and aerial survey has yet to reveal any marching camps up the Highland glens.

DATING THE OCCUPATION OF ELGINHAUGH

Because the historical context of Flavian forts in north Britain is supposedly known from Tacitus' *Agricola* (see above), the archaeological dating evidence from these sites has rarely been assessed in its own right. Indeed, there has been a strong tendency towards circular reasoning so that, having assigned a date to sites and their associated artefacts on historical grounds, the 'dated' artefacts are then taken to confirm the historical date of the site. But even with the relative precision of dating Roman artefacts, it is always going to be difficult on purely archaeological grounds to establish foundation dates for forts in north Britain which may have been built only five or six years apart.

At Elginhaugh, however, we are extremely fortunate in having very good independent dating evidence, particularly from the coin finds and especially from the coin hoard, which was a remarkable and highly unusual find. This is the first Scottish hoard that can be assigned with certainty to the first century AD and one of only five Roman coin hoards recovered in Scotland during the last half century. Most importantly and even more unusually, the hoard was recovered under controlled archaeological conditions, rather than unceremoniously removed without reference to the details of its archaeological context by a digger driver or a metal detector user. As we shall see shortly, that context is crucial to the interpretation and significance of the hoard. It consisted of 45 silver *denarii*, of which more than half (some 25) were worn or much worn Republican *denarii* ranging in date from 115-114 BC to 40 BC (*colour plate 5*). The earliest of the coins would have been almost 200 years old when they were put into the hoard and, apart from two coins minted for Julius Caesar in 46-45 BC, no two coins are alike. The hoard also contains ten of the very common legionary *denarii* of Mark Antony, which are similarly worn or much worn, and again there is no certain duplication amongst them. The last ten coins in the hoard are imperial *denarii*. The earliest is a late issue of Nero, seven pieces are from the reign of Vespasian struck between AD 69 and 71, and the two latest coins were struck by Vespasian for his younger son Domitian, the earlier in AD 74-5 and the second in AD 77-8. The makeup of the hoard is, therefore, somewhat unusual, with a majority of rather elderly Republican issues and an odd group of imperial pieces, with almost no coins duplicated. This suggests that they had been specially selected for inclusion in the hoard, rather than it representing a random cross-section of what happened to be in circulation at the time of deposition.

8 Coins from the hoard *in situ*, stacked one on top of another, in the construction trench of the south wall of the headquarters building (*principia*)

The context of their discovery is similarly significant. The coins were found in three groups, but in such close proximity to each other that they must originally have constituted a single deposit. The first group of 21 coins (*8*) were neatly stacked towards the bottom of a construction trench in the headquarters building, the second group of 23 coins lay on the ground surface on the edge of that trench just inside the building spread over an area no more than 0.3m sq and the third, consisting of a single coin, lay directly above the second in a demolition layer from the systematic dismantling of the building and burning of its wattle and daub walls. Artefacts of any kind are not often retrieved from the construction trenches for timber buildings, but when they are, they usually derive from the demolition process. The removal of posts inevitably disturbs the filling and broken or discarded material from the clearing out of the buildings then finds its way into the tops of trenches. The demolition of the front wall of the headquarters building when the fort was abandoned had certainly partly disturbed the hoard, bringing more than half of it to the surface where it went unnoticed before being covered by demolition debris. But the remainder was sufficiently undisturbed to indicate that it was in its original position near the bottom of the construction trench.

Moreover, such a hoard is unlikely be have been an accidental loss, either during the construction of the fort or its demolition, since it represented approximately one sixth of the annual pay of a cavalry trooper. You might not notice losing £1, or at least not worry too much about it, but you would certainly be aware of losing a few thousand pounds should you ever be carrying such a large sum around with you. Nor does its find-spot in a construction trench at the front of the headquarters building suggest a personal hiding place; the location would have been too public in a busy fort to secrete away your savings. Thus, such a valuable hoard at the front of the main administrative building at almost the exact centre of the fort would seem to indicate some form of official foundation deposit. Ritual deposits in similar locations associated with the building of forts at this period are not unknown elsewhere. A pit containing a deposit of unidentifiable carbonised material was found almost at the centre of the headquarters building of the Roman auxiliary fort founded around AD 80 at Pen Llystyn, Caernarvonshire, and was interpreted as a ritual deposit made at the foundation of the fort. A similar explanation is given for the pit discovered in the centre of the courtyard of the headquarters building of the contemporary legionary fortress at Inchtuthil, Perthshire, which contained charcoal and a small quantity of cremated bone. Finally, the remains of a supposed temporary altar were unearthed at the centre of the auxiliary fort built at the Saalburg in Germany during Domitian's campaign of AD 83 or shortly thereafter.

But, even if the arguments that it was a deliberate, formal ritual deposit are not accepted, there was no evidence that the coins had been placed in the wall trench other than at the time when the building was constructed. While it might be argued that any trace of later interference with the foundations to bury the hoard would have been erased by the demolition process, the fact that over 20 of the coins were found in neat piles indicates that not all traces of their original deposition had been subsequently removed. Furthermore, the very fact that the hoard had been partly disturbed during the demolition process and was not recovered suggests that its presence had already been long forgotten. Accordingly, we may confidently assert on the basis of the coin evidence alone that the headquarters building and, therefore, the fort was constructed not long after AD 78, since the latest dated coin in the hoard is a *denarius* of Vespasian of AD 77/8. Since that coin was only slightly worn, the date of its deposition is unlikely to have been long delayed after its minting.

This foundation date is entirely in accord with the more fragile and generally more closely dateable artefactual material from the site, such as pottery and glass. Almost all the decorated samian pottery is likely to have been made in the AD 70s or early 80s. There are a few pieces that might be described as Neronian-Flavian, that is spanning the period between the later part of the reign of Nero and the early part of the Flavian dynasty, but only one which is certainly of pre-Flavian manufacture. Almost all of the plainware is of Flavian or Neronian-Flavian manufacture, with only one certainly Neronian sherd. Similarly, the date ranges of the stamped and other more closely dateable mortaria or mixing bowls generally fall within the brackets AD 50-85, 60-90+ or 65-110. Again there are at least two vessels which appear to be pre-Flavian forms, though both seem likely to be of local manufacture (see chapter six) and to represent the continued production of an older typological form, rather than pots which had been in use for a lengthy period. Most of the forms and colours in the glass assemblage are typical of the tablewares in circulation in Britain in the AD 70s and 80s, though some vessels are more characteristic of the preceding Claudian and Neronian periods. Finally, though generally less closely dateable, the coarseware pottery assemblage would suggest that the commencement of occupation at the site fell closer to AD 80 than to AD 70 on the one hand, or to AD 90 on the other, but includes a number of fineware types with pre-Flavian associations, such as Lyon ware. Thus, all the pottery and the glass tell a similar story of mid-Flavian occupation, but with slight hints of earlier material.

The presence of a number of Republican *denarii* amongst the site finds has no dating significance, for it is well known that these silver coins had a very long circulation life until they were recalled in the early second century AD. Lower denomination brass or copper coinage, generally referred to as *aes*, did not have the same longevity of use. Nonetheless, the same principle concerning the survival of occasional pieces of 'early' pottery and glass discussed above also applies to the occasional pre-Flavian or early Flavian *aes* coinage from sites in Scotland. Indeed, it is a statistical commonplace that losses at any one time will continue strongly to reflect coin issues of the immediately preceding periods, since more of these are in circulation, the numbers decreasing gradually over time. Nor, indeed, were these lower denomination coins minted, or at least supplied to Britain, in equal numbers each year; rather we see periods when there is a massive injection of coins into circulation interspersed with periods of sporadic supply. Two of the three main periods of substantial supply in the Flavian period were AD 71-3 and AD 77-8, while in the reign of Nero it was the years AD 64-67. In the absence of other coinage coming in to fill the gap, it should not be surprising to find that coins from these three episodes continued in circulation for some time. Thus, the presence of three *aes* coins of Nero (covering the period AD 64-68) and at least six of Vespasian dated to AD 71-3 in the site finds from Elginhaugh should occasion no surprise, despite its slightly later foundation date, and casts serious doubt on any suggestion that small numbers of *aes* coins of similar date from other fort sites in Lowland Scotland and beyond should be taken to indicate a foundation date during the governorship of Petillius Cerialis.

The foundation date of Elginhaugh in AD 79/80 during the governorship of Gaius Julius Agricola should carry with it all of the Flavian forts to the south as far as Corbridge, Red House (see *5*), the latter previously identified as a base for campaigns into Scotland. Recent suggestions that it too may have been an earlier foundation, seem to be based on similar arguments about the presence of limited amounts of early Flavian material and may be discounted on the statistical grounds already outlined.

Although there are clear traces of a second structural phase in the men's accommodation in several of the barrack blocks (nos 1, 2, 3, 4, 5 and 6) (see *25, 27* and *29*), this does not seem to constitute a major reconstruction of the fort, for only relatively minor remodelling of the interiors of the relevant barracks is involved (chapter four) and the central range shows no sign of more than one structural phase. Similarly, the second phase attested in two of the gates seems to be no more than reconstruction after temporary blocking, the latter probably for purely local reasons perhaps related to a minor realignment of Dere Street so that it avoided passing through the middle of the fort.

Narrow, straight-sided slots were cut across each portal at both front and rear of the east gate (*9*). These clearly postdated the erection of the gate superstructure, for they cut

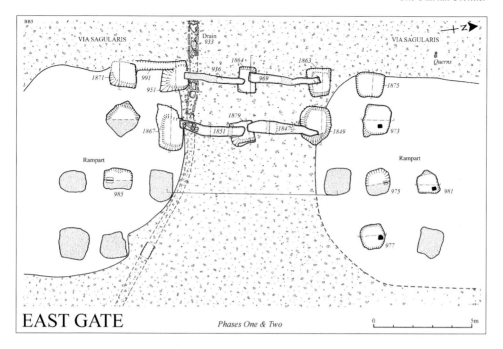

EAST GATE

Phases One & Two

9 Plan of the east gate: phases 1 & 2

the six backfilled primary post pits that defined the entrance and the drain. Superficially they resemble slots for threshold beams, which housed the vertical pivots on which the doors were hung, but these should be located only at the front of the entrance portal. More fundamentally, however, the slots are far too deep and irregular. Threshold beam slots need have been no deeper than the cross-section of the beams they contained, of the order of 0.2-0.3m, as was the case at the south gate where the slot was no more than 0.28m deep. With one exception, these secondary slots at the east gate ranged in depth from 0.61m to 1.32m and seem to indicate the deliberate blocking of the entrance. After an uncertain, but probably brief, period of time the gateway was recommissioned. The six post pits that formed the passageway across the entrance gap were re-dug, along with the two outer post pits at the rear of the towers, the secondary post pits being consistently shallower and less regular than their primary counterparts. The west gate was less comprehensively excavated, but a possible threshold slot noted in section was too deep (0.63m) and too far forward of the two outer gate posts to have performed that function adequately. On analogy with the east gate, it seems best interpreted as some form of blocking feature, for it clearly cut a primary post pit. Thereafter, both the entrance passage and the whole of the south tower were rebuilt, involving the replacement of thirteen posts (*10*). As in the east gate, the secondary post pits tended to be smaller and less rectilinear in shape than their predecessors, whose positions they mirrored quite closely.

Also, the augmentation of the defences with the possible addition of three ditches around the perimeter of the fort seems more likely to relate to a reassessment of the

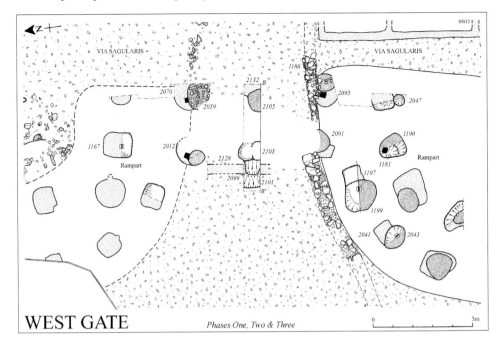

10 Plan of the west gate: phases 1, 2 & 3

security provision than indicative of a second substantive phase of occupation. Though there clearly are two major structural reorganisations in the interior of the annexe during the life of the fort (phases 1b and 1c) (below, chapter five), fluctuations in use of the annexe need not necessarily reflect, or even coincide with, structural phases within the fort. Indeed, both structural reorganisations of the annexe seem to have been relatively short lived and related to the closing years of the occupation, since a *terminus post quem* for the first (phase 1b) is provided by a coin of AD 85 in the makeup of the associated road, indicating that it took place perhaps only a year or two before the abandonment of the fort. Although there would appear to have been a small adjustment to the size of the garrison (below, chapter four), it is difficult to interpret these changes as the local manifestation of the wider strategic re-assessment of the Flavian occupation generally categorised in the modern literature as Flavian II (see below).

A PHASED WITHDRAWAL

That occupation at Elginhaugh did not extend into the last decade of the first century is clearly indicated by the dating evidence recovered, particularly the coins. The latest dated coins from the site are unworn or only slightly worn *sestertii* or *asses* of AD 86 (*11*), a picture not infrequently observed at sites north of the Forth-Clyde isthmus, including Inchtuthil, Stracathro, Strageath and Cardean. The dating significance of these coins has been further reconsidered by Andrew Hobley, who has convincingly asserted that they provide more than just a *terminus post quem* for the cessation of occupation. In fact, it is the absence of coins of AD 87, which are well attested in the civil province as one of the main issues of Domitian circulating in Britain, which indicates that the occupation of Elginhaugh and other sites further north with similar coin finds had ceased before this issue had reached the province. Since the military were usually the first to receive new coin, that would indicate the abandonment of these northern forts by AD 87 or 88.

Withdrawal from the fort at Elginhaugh was clearly a policy decision on the part of the Roman authorities for there is clear, consistent and widespread evidence of deliberate demolition of the fort's internal buildings. Demolition pits filled with burnt daub, charcoal and discarded artefacts were widely distributed across the fort (*colour plate 6*). These often cut through the construction trenches of buildings, presumably to facilitate the removal of timber uprights. Where post impressions survived, as in barrack 2, they frequently showed signs of disturbance, while one of the surviving posts in barrack 3 appeared to have been sawn off. Concentrations of burnt daub and charcoal suggested that the wattle and daub panels of the buildings were collected together and burnt, though in one case, at the west end of barrack 1, the walling had collapsed or been pushed inwards and then partially burnt. The concentration of finds from these demolition contexts suggests that the site was cleared of rubbish in the process. Within the *aedes*, the religious focus of the site at the rear of the headquarters building, the pit which had probably housed the garrison's strong-box was carefully filled and sealed with clay. Finally, after the buildings had been demolished, a shallow pit was dug on the site of barrack 9 to dispose of 165kg of unused nails (*colour plate 7*). The evidence of total and methodical destruction of the external bathhouse is also clear. The walls had been dismantled, the stones thrown to the ground outside and the box flues and plaster let fall within. The subfloor was found to be choked with pillar bricks and tiles, the latter smashed into three or four pieces by a clean blow from some heavy implement.

Similar evidence comes from several forts north of the Forth Clyde isthmus, including the legionary fortress at Inchtuthil and the auxiliary forts at Strageath, Fendoch and Cardean. At Inchtuthil, the timber posts of the buildings were extracted, leaving a scatter of bent nails of all sizes, and the wattle and daub infilling of the walls was collected together and burnt. Glass and pottery from storerooms along the main road through the fortress, the *via principalis*, was dumped into the gutter alongside that road, while nearly ten tons of iron, mainly unused stocks of nails, were buried in a huge pit in the front of the workshop, which was then sealed with gravel to prevent its later discovery and re-use of its contents by the native population. At Strageath, demolition pits had been dug through buildings to dispose of rubbish, there was consistent evidence of burnt daub and charcoal in the tops of construction trenches, where timbers had been extracted, as well as in the drains, one which also contained a lead pig and four iron ingots. At Fendoch, the timbers of the gates and internal buildings had been dug out of their pits and construction trenches, the backfill containing broken and twisted nails, while at Cardean broken pottery and glass had been neatly disposed of in the butt ends of the ditches.

Explanation for this change of policy is to be sought not in Scotland, but much closer to Rome. A serious military setback on the Danube frontier resulted in the withdrawal

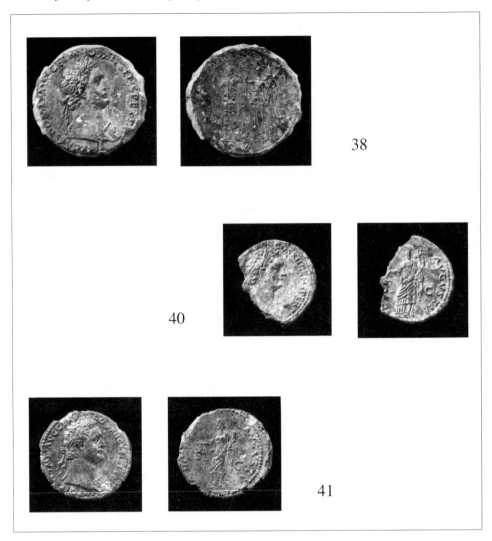

11 Obverse and reverse of unworn/slightly worn *sestertius* (38) and *asses* (40, 43) of Domitian AD 86. *Copyright: Hunterian Museum and Art Gallery, University of Glasgow*

of troops from Britain. The Dacians under Decebalus attacked the Roman province of Moesia in AD 85, killing the governor, Oppius Sabinus, and many of his troops. The emperor Domitian himself travelled to the area with his praetorian prefect, Cornelius Fuscus, to restore peace, but a subsequent, perhaps overconfident, punitive expedition into Dacia under Fuscus met with disaster — he lost his life and his army. At this stage, more troops had to be assembled and detailed preparations made to avenge these serious setbacks, and so it was a further two years, in AD 88, before Decebalus and his Dacian forces were defeated by Tettius Julianus at Tapae, Transylvania's Iron Gates.

The Roman army was no less finite than any other army, and the legions in particular were a limited resource, with only some twenty-nine across the whole of the empire at this time. Though new legions could be recruited, and Domitian did raise one for his war against the Chatti probably in AD 82, this was not achieved as easily as the recruitment of new auxiliary troops and training took some time. Accordingly, military problems or preparations for major campaigns in one area necessitated troop transfers from another. This is the context for the transfer of *legio II Adiutrix* from its base in Chester to the Danube (though it is not directly attested there until AD 92) and the consequent withdrawal of the legionary garrison from Inchtuthil, presumably the *XXth Valeria Victrix*, to fill the gap in northern England. No doubt auxiliary units will have accompanied *legio II Adiutrix* to the Danube. As noted above, manpower had already been stretched by the speed of Roman expansion across north Wales, northern England and into Scotland. As a direct result of this withdrawal of troops from Britain, the Romans failed fully to consolidate the conquest of the north, reminding us of the constraints that shortages of manpower could impose on Rome's expansionist policies. Britain was just one small remote province in a huge empire and decisions which affected it were not necessarily always taken entirely with local considerations in mind.

The exact limit of Roman military occupation and control at this time is not absolutely clear. Withdrawal from forts north of the Forth–Clyde isthmus carried with it sites at least as far south as Elginhaugh in the east and Crawford in the west, both having produced coins of AD 86 as their latest site finds. However, minor discrepancies in the dating evidence from different sites may indicate that the withdrawal was phased rather than entirely synchronous. There are hints in the pottery evidence at Elginhaugh that occupation continued very slightly longer than other sites to the north. The ratio of forms 29 to 37, the main types of decorated samian bowl, is markedly lower than in the Flavian occupations of Camelon, Inchtuthil and Strageath, suggesting that Elginhaugh may have been occupied for slightly longer to allow time to acquire a higher proportion of form 37 after the manufacture of form 29 came to an end (c.AD 85). But it cannot have continued to be garrisoned for longer than a year or two more, given the total absence of the new styles of decoration that came rapidly into use in the later 80s. This may also help to account for the two sherds of plainware that should be categorised as Flavian-Trajanic, the presence of coarse pottery forms attested also at Corbridge Main Site, which was not founded before AD 85 and of several sherds of mortaria with a date range of AD 80-120.

But sustained occupation of forts in Lowland Scotland after AD 86, usually referred to as Flavian II, can be demonstrated confidently only as far north as the key sites at Newstead in the east and Dalswinton in the west (*12*), though in the latter case this is based on structural phases rather than any detailed assessment of the dating evidence. Both forts underwent a major overhaul; already large they were further enlarged, a *terminus post quem* for the rebuilding at the former provided by two *aes* coins of AD 86 in almost mint condition recovered from the infilled ditches of the earlier fort.

Nonetheless, some level of Roman control and influence seems to have extended beyond these installations, though direct evidence of this has only been brought to light by the excavations at Elginhaugh. After the buildings within the auxiliary fort were demolished, the enclosure formed by the rampart continued to be used as a collection

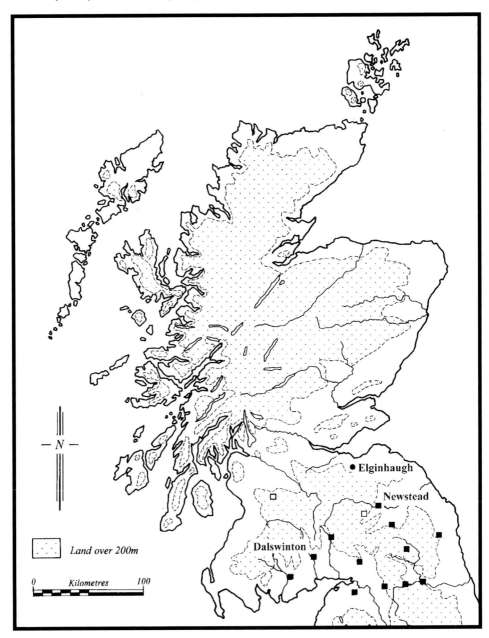

12 Distribution map of late Flavian forts in north Britain

point for animals, presumably as part of the exaction of tribute from the area (see chapter seven for a full discussion of the evidence for this interpretation). This might be taken to imply that the fort was given up before the late 80s AD. However, with one exception, all the latest dated coins recovered derive from general demolition spreads, or from upper layers disturbed by post-Roman ploughing, suggesting that they had been lost during the demolition process. The exception, a very slightly worn *as* possibly of AD 85, contained in the makeup of a road of phase 1b in the annexe already alluded to above and would indicate occupation continuing until at least the following year.

Exactly how long this limited occupation of Lowland Scotland continued is uncertain, but within less than 20 years even the forts beyond the Tyne–Solway isthmus were abandoned. The closely dateable samian pottery from the two large sites at Newstead and Dalswinton suggests that their occupation did not extend for more than five years or so beyond the turn of the first century. Once again the withdrawal was probably brought about by the demands of an extensive military commitment beyond the Danube in Dacia, this time as the emperor Trajan sought the conquest of that area, beginning his first campaign in AD 103. Once again this appears to have been a deliberate withdrawal, though the evidence is more equivocal than that from AD 87/8. Several forts have produced evidence of burning which has previously been interpreted as indicative of enemy action. In most cases more detailed examination does not sustain this interpretation, and in one case, at Carlisle, where extensive excavation and the waterlogged conditions have allowed the retrieval of detailed structural evidence, there is no doubt that the buildings were demolished before being rebuilt. At Corbridge, however, there does appear to have been a more extensive and uncontrolled fire before the rebuilding, the latter dated to some time after AD 103 on the basis of a coin of Trajan from a construction trench in one of the barracks of the second period fort. So the area may have become troublesome at the same time as troops were needed elsewhere, resulting in the re-drawing of the limit of Roman military control across the Tyne-Solway isthmus, usually referred to as the Trajanic or Stanegate frontier. It is ironic that it was Trajan, the most expansionist ruler that the empire had seen since the days of Augustus himself, who was responsible for the abandonment of the last vestiges of the Flavian conquest of Scotland. But it serves to emphasise again the relatively low strategic importance of a Britain at the northern limit of Roman territory, compared to the provinces on either side of the Danube which lay at the heart of Rome's European empire.

THREE

MILITARY BUILDERS

Roman military installations can be conveniently divided into a number of types. Legionary bases or fortresses were large, up to 50 acres (20ha) in internal area, to provide sufficient space to house the 5000 citizen infantry troops, which constituted a legion. Auxiliary units, made up of non-citizen troops, were much smaller, generally *c.*500-1000 men, either infantry, cavalry or, most commonly, a mixture of the two and their forts varied in size from some 2 acres (0.8ha) to over 12 acres (4.9ha) in internal area, though, as we shall see (below, chapter four), there is no easy correlation between auxiliary fort size and garrison type. Much smaller installations that lack an independent headquarters building and are provided with only one or two gates are also frequently attested. These fortlets can vary greatly in internal area from less than 0.1 acre (0.04ha) to *c.*1 acre (0.4ha), though there is a potential grey area between large fortlets and small forts when the character of the internal buildings is not known.

The Roman army was clearly responsible for building all its own military installations, as abundant epigraphic evidence makes clear for later periods. We even have preserved in two late historical sources, the writings of Vegetius and the Digest of Justinian, lists of craftsmen employed in the army, including surveyors, architects, glaziers, smiths, carpenters and others trained in construction work. The detailed evidence available from Elginhaugh lets us consider a number of issues ranging from the building methods employed and the way the process was organised, to the types of buildings constructed, how they might have looked in three dimensions and how often they needed to be repaired.

METHODS AND MATERIALS

It was standard practice in Britain in the first century AD, as it was on the contemporary German frontier, to build forts in timber with a surrounding rampart of turf or clay. So it was at Elginhaugh, in both the fort and the annexe, where we see two of the three standard timber building techniques employed. Careful recording of this evidence can provide important clues about not only the building process, but also concerning the likely three-dimensional appearance of the buildings.

Post hole construction, where individual holes were dug for single posts, was employed as the sole method of construction only for gates and towers. This structural choice seems to be dictated by two requirements: the spacing of major structural supports at intervals at least two to three times greater than the average in timber buildings, which is usually less than 1m, and the need to provide deeper foundations for increased load-bearing capacity. Under these circumstances it would be wasteful of time and energy to dig a continuous trench rather than individual post holes. Thus, the gates were constructed using large uprights up to 3.35m apart, usually rectangular in cross section, averaging 0.22 x 0.24m, though with considerable variation (*colour plate 8*). Such dimensions for the posts are slightly below those generally recorded in first century forts elsewhere in Britain. The posts were set in large, usually sub-rectangular, pits up to 2m across and 1.55m deep, though here again there was considerable variation with a noticeable tendency for secondary post pits to be shallower and less regular (*colour plate 9*). In the annexe, the gate post holes were smaller and much shallower than those in the fort, being sub-circular or sub-rectangular in plan with maximum dimensions of 1.36m across and less than 1m in depth, though the posts they contained were of similar size. The interval and corner towers in the fort were similarly constructed, though the posts were more frequently square in section and the interval tower posts slightly smaller, averaging 0.21m x 0.23m. The post pits were generally square and, again like the posts themselves, slightly smaller than those for the gates, up to 1.26m across and 1.3m deep (*colour plate 10*).

Elsewhere in the fort, posts set within post holes were used to support internal ambulatories or colonnades, as in the commanding officer's house and the headquarters building (see *18* and *20*). Though not reaching the dimensions of gate and tower post pits, those in the headquarters building were up to 0.75m deep, and 1.4m across. The examples in the commanding officer's house averaged only 0.4m deep, though were of similar surface dimensions. The few recorded examples of post impressions, indications of where the actual posts had been left to rot *in situ* or been pulled out and the resultant holes infilled with different material, indicate that the post holes contained large uprights between 0.23 and 0.37m in cross-section. Finally, individual post holes were also employed along the sides of the granaries between each transverse post trench to provide additional support for a suspended floor (*21* and *colour plate 11*). This is a unique structural feature, though paralleled in general principle in the contemporary forts at Pen Llystyn and Cardean. The only other structure in the fort in which post hole construction was employed, other than for repairs, was in the inner wall of the southern suite of the officers' quarters in barracks 3 and 4.

Post hole construction was slightly more widely used in the buildings in the annexe than it was in the fort. Post holes were sometimes used in combination with post trenches, either across the front of buildings or to define internal divisions, and in one case (building F) they appeared to outline the entire building, spaced at intervals of between 2m to 3.5m (see *40*). Finally, even more widely spaced post holes were used to support a rail fence. The post holes were mainly circular and quite small, usually of the order of 0.4-0.5m or less. Some, notably in building F, were stone packed, but post impressions were rare. Post hole depths did not tend to exceed 0.5m, and most were of 0.3–0.4m, though as with many of the post trenches there had been much truncation by the plough.

With the above exceptions, all the other buildings in the fort were built using post trenches, which is by far the most common method of construction employed in first-century Roman forts. This involves digging continuous trenches which define the building plan and placing free-standing posts within them at regular intervals. The post trenches varied considerably in size. Widths of between 0.2m and 0.9m were recorded, but outer or other load-bearing wall trenches were generally between 0.3m and 0.5m wide, while partition walls were consistently narrower, usually within the range 0.2–0.4m. The major exceptions were the massive inner office walls at the rear end of the headquarters building, the likely significance of which in terms of reconstruction of that building are discussed below. The recorded depth of the construction trenches varied enormously across the fort, from as little as 0.1m to almost ten times that depth, but little significance can be attached to such figures in general because of the varying levels of truncation of the remains across the excavated area. Where original depths were recorded, as in barracks 7 and 9, figures of 0.75m and 0.96m were indicated for outer load-bearing walls. What was clear, however, was that inner, non load-bearing wall trenches were considerably shallower. This was particularly apparent in barrack 10, the only building in the fort whose construction trenches were entirely emptied, where a marked depth differentiation of up to 0.2m was noted at the junctions between the partition and load-bearing walls (*colour plate 12*).

Sleeper-beam construction, whereby a horizontal beam was placed directly on the ground surface or in a shallow trench and uprights morticed into it in the manner of a medieval timber-framed building, is sometimes postulated in first-century AD forts, but is identified more often than the evidence justifies because of a consistent failure on the part of excavators adequately to distinguish it from post-trench construction. None of the construction trenches within the fort at Elginhaugh had the characteristics of sleeper-beam construction. The trenches were of varying depth and, allowing for later truncation, consistently too deep. They were sometimes discontinuous and irregular in alignment. Though post impressions were infrequently recorded, sufficient were noted to indicate that they penetrated to the bottom, or even occasionally below the bottom, of the construction trenches. All these features are incompatible with the use of sleeper beams.

Where post impressions were noted in the internal buildings, or posts survived, they showed considerable variation in dimensions, best exemplified in barracks 3 and 4. Most of the posts were square or rectangular, usually between 0.1m and 0.2m in cross-section, with some indication from barracks 9 and 10 of slightly larger posts in load-bearing walls. The major exceptions were the post impressions in the granary trenches and post holes, which were consistently circular. This is a common feature in granaries, reflecting the survival of evidence relating to the construction of the subfloor rather than the superstructure. The significance of the use of circular posts in relation to the reconstruction of the granaries is discussed below.

A number of posts had clearly penetrated the bottom of the construction trenches. This was recorded in the commanding officer's house, the granaries and barrack 10. This may indicate later subsidence, but seems more likely to have been deliberate, in order to give greater stability to the posts and more readily fix them in position during the construction process. Certainly two of the extant repair posts in barrack 3 had their ends sharpened to a wedge shape so that they might be driven into the bottom of the trench. On the other hand, the penetration of posts below the bottom of the construction trench was not universally recorded and other extant posts from barrack 3 had flat bottoms. In addition, stone slabs were noted at the bottom of the trench, as if to provide additional support and prevent subsidence.

Insufficient examples of posts or post impressions survived to indicate the spacing between them. In granaries it is assumed to mirror the 1.5m spacing between the parallel construction trenches in order to produce a regular pattern of supports for the raised floor. In other buildings, however, the posts recorded would have formed the main wall supports and closer spacing would have been required. A spacing of 0.9m was recorded in one of the repair trenches in barrack 3, which fits the norm recorded in military timber buildings.

Infilling between the uprights was consistently of wattle and daub, a mixture of clay and straw. Daub was recorded in some form, most frequently in demolition deposits, in association with every internal building in the fort except the granaries. Sometimes the daub was well preserved by burning. Some fifty pieces were recovered from the annexe and over 220 from the fort. Some twenty-one of the latter preserved impressions of the wattles, which were usually some 15mm in diameter, though one example was twice that size. This compares closely with the wattles from the wells (*colour plate 13*), which were mainly between 9mm and 22mm in diameter. In three or four places where major repairs had been necessary, or the demolition was less thorough, further structural details were recovered. In the south-west corner of the commanding officer's house, a stub of walling had been sealed by a demolition spread, indicating the original wall width of 0.3-0.4m, while charcoal samples from a pit in barrack 7 and from the collapsed end wall of barrack 1 indicate wattles of 20mm and 15mm in diameter respectively.

Because of the waterlogging of parts of the site, caused by silt/clay bands within the glacial sands, additional structural details were preserved in some of the gates and towers and one of the barrack buildings. Of the three extant timbers in the north and south gates, only one was oak (*colour plate 8*), usually the most commonly attested species. The other two were of alder. Similarly, the only two surviving timbers from two interval towers were both of alder. All five uprights preserved in a repair trench in barrack 3 were alder, with hazel, alder, birch and willow used for wattling.

Although there is some evidence of structural carpentry, including a very fine grooved alder beam discarded in the well in the *principia* during the construction of the fort, the buildings are likely to have been put together with the liberal use of iron nails. These were the most abundant metal artefact type recovered, usually found singly and widely scattered across the site. In the majority of cases, they were so badly corroded that further analysis was not worthwhile. However, a cache of 160.5kg of nails (*colour plate 7*), corroded together into a single mass, had been deposited in a demolition pit. Some 1362 separate nails were extracted, though the vast majority of these were fragmentary, and detailed examination facilitated an estimate of the total number present as approximately 29,000. None of the nails were bent, indicating that they were probably unused, and the overwhelming majority were small, with lengths between 38 and 70mm, suggesting that they may have been primarily unused stock from roof repairs.

Unusually for a first-century fort, one of the internal buildings was, in part at least, constructed in stone. The only other attested example of mortared stone construction in a Flavian fort in Scotland is the addition of a stone face to the turf rampart of the legionary fortress at Inchtuthil, though stone is common in the construction of bath buildings outside timber-built forts, as attested at Elginhaugh itself. These two specific examples encapsulate many of the reasons for the employment of stone: for additional security and strengthened defences; for greater status and prestige for important buildings; and for increased fire resistance; to which must be added the most usually inferred aspect, greater permanence. Of these reasons, only the third, increased fire resistance, seems to provide any reasonable explanation for the use of stone in what has been interpreted as a *fabrica* or workshop at Elginhaugh (see *22* and *colour plate 14*). However, the building represented only the minimum use of stone, for the turf rampart of the fort formed the fourth wall, revetted by timber posts, while the stone walling itself was probably restricted to footings. The presence of one possible post setting within the wall and the abundant evidence of charcoal and burnt daub in the vicinity suggest that the superstructure was of timber.

Such half-timbered construction in Roman forts is assumed more often than it can be proven, so it is worthwhile to note some details of the construction. The footings were of mortared sandstone, 0.7-0.8m wide, and up to 0.5m in height from surviving floor levels. One possible post setting suggested that the timber superstructure was tied into the wall by bedding uprights within it, though these did not penetrate to ground level. The construction trench for the wall was quite shallow, only 0.31-0.45m deep. On the evidence currently available, it does not seem likely that any of the bathhouse was of part-timbered construction. Interestingly, however, the clay-mortared walls were actually of smaller width than those in the workshop, rarely exceeding 0.6m, with the partition walls even narrower.

FORT LAYOUT

It is commonly assumed that Roman forts were so standardised that their plans are well known; that the same buildings were built to the same plans in the same locations within different forts. Indeed, so prevalent was this view of the predictability of fort plans thirty or more years ago that it was not felt necessary to excavate more than a sample of a fort site to allow the reconstruction of the whole plan. The classic example of this is Ian Richmond's excavations at the Flavian auxiliary fort at Fendoch in Perthshire in the 1930s, a direct parallel to Elginhaugh both geographically and chronologically. The published fort plan was subsequently widely reproduced as an example of a typical

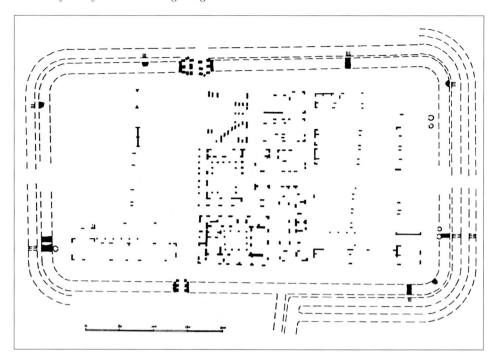

13 Plan of the Agricolan fort at Fendoch showing the area actually excavated

timber-built fort, but closer examination indicates how little of the site was actually excavated (*13*). Clearly, if subsequent fort plans are extrapolated on the basis of a plan which itself is heavily restored, the standardisation of Roman fort plans becomes a self-fulfilling prophesy. Indeed, it was belief in this standardisation that led to the suggestion that fort buildings were actually prefabricated and transported to new sites to be erected rather like larger versions of modern flat-packed furniture. Such a belief influenced the famous full-scale reconstructions of a timber gate and granary at the Lunt, in Baginton near Coventry in the early 1970s (*colour plate 15*). In recent decades, however, it has become increasingly apparent that all Roman forts are different, as we might expect since they were built by different units for different garrisons at different times.

Yet, at the same time, forts were built by, and for, the military to serve the same or similar purposes wherever they were established. As such it should not be surprising that, at least from the Flavian period onwards, they show a remarkable consistency of design and layout, indicating adherence to a number of general principles. These were in force also at Elginhaugh (*14*). The famous playing-card shape, rectangular with rounded corners, is clearly in evidence, with four double-portal gates in the centre of each side, though this positioning is more common in forts of square than those of rectangular plan. Six-post guard towers were set within the rampart at each corner, with further four-post examples filling the gap between these and the gates, thus providing towers at regular intervals around the perimeter.

The fort was defined by a rampart *c.*6.5m wide on average at its base, with inturned entrances. In the best-preserved section to the east of the south gate, the rampart was

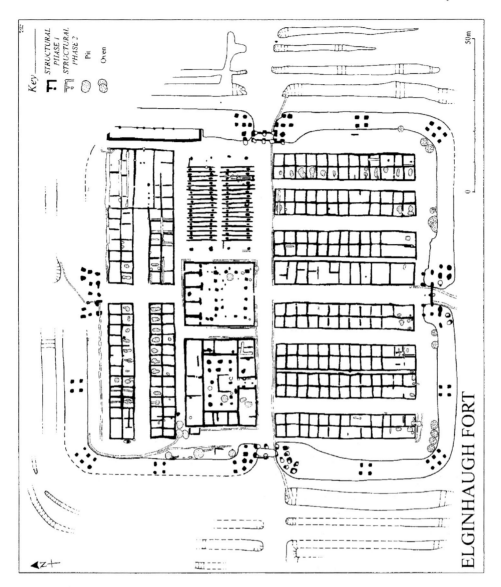

14 Elginhaugh: overall plan of the fort

revetted with turf cheeks 2.6-2.8m wide at both front and rear, the core of the rampart infilled with mixed soil and turf. On the west side of the fort to the south of the main road, however, the rampart appeared to consist entirely of clay (*colour plate 10*). Originally the fort was surrounded by multiple ditches, though in its final form possibly only by one. These external defences were exposed in their entirety only in the south-east quadrant to the south of Dere Street, where four ditches were present, and sampling suggested that this number may have varied only slightly elsewhere around the perimeter. For example, though only three ditches are attested on the north side of the fort, a fourth may have been provided by the continuation of the annexe ditch. However, only two were provided on the east side immediately north of the main through road, and given the proximity of a steep scarp slope on the south side, any extensive additional man-made provision would seem to have been superfluous, though this could not be tested within the area available for excavation. The inner ditch, at between 3m and 5.75m in width and up to 2.15m deep, was consistently the largest of those surrounding the fort, usually by a considerable margin, though in part this may have been the result of later re-cutting (15). Most of the ditches had standard, broad V-shaped profiles with basal slots or channels, though in few cases were these sharply defined. Traditionally these slots, which are commonly attested at Roman fort sites, have been interpreted as designed to augment the defensive potential of the ditches by increasing the likelihood of an assailant breaking an ankle as he attempted to cross. But this interpretation has little to commend it, for a sharply defined V-shape could have had the same effect, and they are best interpreted as a constructional feature linked to the need to allow room to manoeuvre when digging out the bottom of a steep-sided ditch, perhaps being augmented by the later regular cleaning out of any accumulated silts.

Confusingly, the internal areas of Roman forts can be calculated in one of three ways according to the level of information available for individual sites: either within the ditches (often used for sites known only from aerial reconnaissance), over the ramparts or within the ramparts, the latter equating most closely to the area available for buildings. This variation in practice can make comparisons between sites difficult, particularly as it can result in differences of as much as 33 per cent for the same site. The relevant measurements for Elginhaugh are *c.*4.6 acres (1.85ha), 3.85 acres (1.56ha) and 3.26 acres (1.32ha). Whatever the mode of measurement, however, Elginhaugh may reasonably be referred to as a relatively small auxiliary fort.

The standard arrangement of roads is also evident (14). The *via principalis,* 6.5m wide, ran between the east and west gates, bisecting the fort and forming a T-junction with the *via praetoria* immediately in the front of the *principia (colour plate 2)*. The 5.5m wide *via praetoria* would have been nominally the main road into the fort, indicating that it faced south, but the south gate was inconveniently situated on the edge of a steep scarp overlooking the river. Clearly, the *via principalis* must have served as the main thoroughfare and was, in fact, a continuation of Dere Street, the main north–south Roman arterial route into Scotland up the east side of the country. Outside the fort to the east, immediately beyond the outer ditch, the line of this road widened and veered to the north, possibly heading for a more convenient crossing of the North Esk, perhaps in the vicinity of the modern bridge. To the west it continued through the main annexe, swinging very slightly to the north as it passed through the ditches before returning to its original alignment. At the rear of the fort the gap between the ends of the barracks suggests that the *via decumana*, running from the north gate to the *principia*, would have been up to 6m in width, but only occasional patches of metalling survived the plough. The intervallum road mirrored the inside of the rampart all around the fort. Though nominally as much as 7m wide in places, various constrictions reduced this width. As a result it would have been difficult to take a wheeled vehicle continuously around the

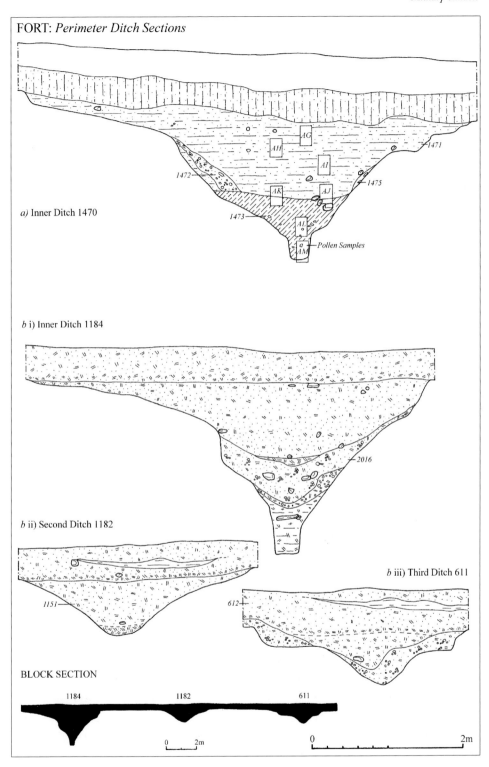

FORT: *Perimeter Ditch Sections*

a) Inner Ditch 1470

b i) Inner Ditch 1184

b ii) Second Ditch 1182

b iii) Third Ditch 611

BLOCK SECTION

15 Ditch sections on north and west sides of the fort

perimeter. The inward projection of the rampart at all four gates reduced the width of the intervallum road to as little as *c.*1.4m on the southern side of the west gate, and to *c.*3-4m at the north gate and on the southern side of the east gate. Despite the fact that the rampart had been cut back to accommodate it, the workshop narrowed the adjacent road to 2.3m in the north-east corner (see *22*), while the ovens in the south-east and south-west corners reduced passage to a width of *c.*3.5m and 2.5m respectively.

Thus, the overall layout of the fort was very compact, not to say cramped. Though emphasis has been placed on the potential restrictions to movement, access to all parts of the fort by vehicular traffic would still have been relatively straightforward, even if it involved passing between facing barracks. It is particularly noticeable that, both in terms of location and the provision of roads, ready access to, and free flow of movement around, the granaries were assured.

The standard tripartite division of the fort interior is maintained (*14*), with the commanding officer's house and granaries in the central range lying to the north of the *via principalis*. Behind them were barracks, two on either side of the *via decumana*, arranged across the width of the fort running parallel with the north rampart. On the other side of the *via principalis* were the rest of the barracks and a single store building (no. 8), arranged parallel to the long axis of the fort, on either side of the *via praetoria*. In all cases, the officers' quarters appear to lie at the outer end, closest to the rampart, which is common practice. Located beyond the intervallum road against the rear of the rampart at irregular intervals were ovens and occasional working areas. These were positioned there so as to minimise the danger of fire to the wooden buildings in the interior. Thus, the general layout of the fort offers few surprises and can be readily paralleled in numerous auxiliary forts of the first to third centuries throughout the Roman Empire.

GATES AND TOWERS

Each gate was double portalled and provided with flanking towers, which projected in front of the gate portals; a basic design which is commonly attested in Flavian and earlier auxiliary forts in both Britain and Germany. However, three of the gates (south, east and west) were additionally and uniquely provided with forward extensions to these towers, which served to continue the gate structure to the front of the rampart (see *9*, *10*, *16* and *colour plate 9*). This thickened or turned inwards at each entrance, completely filling the base of each tower. Such an arrangement is not readily paralleled in Britain, though is reminiscent of the more elaborate L-shaped gateways of Augustan date in Germany, such as Haltern. Access to the towers and rampart top was by means of ramps (*ascensus*). One was provided at each gate, attested by the thickening of the rampart to the left-hand side as viewed from the interior of the fort. The six-post towers on each side of the gates were not regular rectangles but splayed outwards mirroring the curve of the rampart. Except at the north gate, the six posts which defined the passageway formed a regular rectangle. There was, however, some considerable variation in the width of the individual portals. The width of the eastern portal of the south gate, as measured

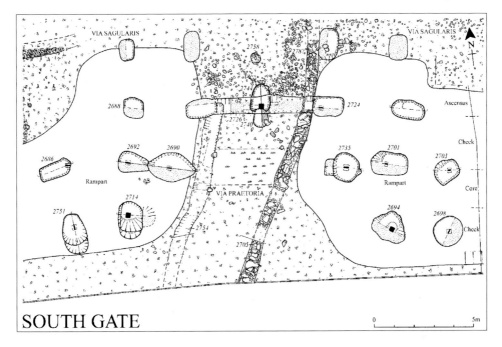

SOUTH GATE

0   5m

16 Plan of the south gate

between the inside edges of the post impressions, was 2.75m; the equivalent distance in the north gate was 3.4m. A threshold trench, originally some 0.4m wide and 0.28m deep, though subsequently disturbed and enlarged, was recorded running across the outer portals of the south gate (*16*).

The size of the timbers involved and the depth of the post pits into which they were set clearly indicates that the gate superstructure was intended to rise to a considerable height. On analogy with the interval and corner towers (below), whose construction would have been entirely superfluous unless they provided a further storey above the top of the rampart, a three-storey structure is assumed. The illustrations of gates on Trajan's Column provide general confirmation that this was the case. A total height of 7-8m is assumed. This allows some 3-3.5m for the height of the gate, sufficient to allow loaded wagons or mounted cavalry troops to enter; a further 2.5-3m for the second storey to provide adequate room for spears to be wielded freely; and another 1.5m for the railing on the third storey. Major debate then revolves around the extent to which the gate superstructure was enclosed and roofed. Following Trajan's Column, most reconstructions take a minimalist approach with neither roofing nor infilling between the uprights, other than simple cross bracing, except for the continuation through the gate of the parapet on top of the rampart (*colour plate 15*). In all cases, the bases of the towers were contained within the rampart so that no guard chambers would have been provided at ground level. The position of the door would have been at the front of the entrance portal. The discovery of threshold slots, as for example at the south gate at Elginhaugh (*16*), or of the surviving beam in the case of Carlisle (*colour plate 16*), tends

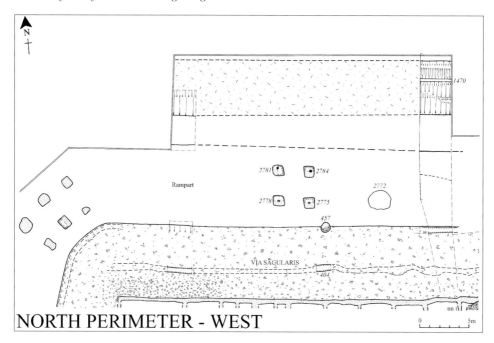

NORTH PERIMETER - WEST

17 Plan of the north-west corner tower and north-north-west interval tower

to confirm this. The primary function of the threshold beam was to house vertical pivots into which the doors were set. To have placed the door at the rear of the gate would have considerably reduced the defensive capability of the gateway by providing a protected refuge beneath the superstructure for any attacker who got sufficiently close to take advantage of it.

As the name implies, corner towers were situated at each of the four corners of the fort (see *14*). There would have been two interval towers along each side of the fort, situated approximately midway between corner tower and gate. Three of the four corner towers and five of the eight interval towers were uncovered in whole or in part, though not all of their exposed post pits were excavated. The towers were all set within the body of the fort rampart, which made them difficult to detect. Where their relative positions could be established, the front posts were set back some 1.6-2.5m from the front of the rampart. The corner towers were sub-rectangular, six-post structures, the posts set in a chevron pattern to follow the curve of the rampart (*17* and *colour plate 17*). Insufficient post impressions were evident to allow precise dimensions of the towers to be given but, assuming that the posts were centrally located within their pits, they would have measured 6.0-6.2m x 2.7-3.3m externally. In the one example, in the south-west tower, where post impressions were identified, a width of 2.8m was recorded. In one case, in the north-west corner, the distance between the inner three posts pits was over a metre less than between the outer three, which would have resulted in a slightly fan- or wedge-shaped tower. The interval towers were simple, approximately square, four-post structures. The greater number of post impressions noted allowed more precise dimensions to be recorded in two cases, the west–south–west and north–north–west towers (*17*), where the external dimensions were almost exactly 3.3m in both directions.

INTERNAL BUILDING TYPES AND THEIR RECONSTRUCTION

The headquarters building or *principia* faced almost exactly due south fronting onto the *via principalis* and measured externally 23.6m x 21m (*18* and *colour plate 18*). Its identification was clear from both its central position within the fort and its morphology, for its tripartite division is typical of such buildings. The best parallels for the overall plan are provided, not surprisingly, by the broadly contemporary timber headquarters buildings from the forts at Pen Llystyn, Fendoch and Strageath (*19*), though no two plans are exactly the same. The front entrance opened into a courtyard, surrounded by a post-defined ambulatory, which took up some 50 per cent of the building. In one corner of the courtyard was a well surrounded by a tripod arrangement of posts presumably to support some form of lifting device. The well was wattle lined with hazel and alder wattles still preserved by waterlogging towards the bottom (*colour plate 13*). Beyond the courtyard was the cross hall with its tribunal or raised dais at one end, where the commanding officer could address assembled troops. Finally, at the rear was a range of five offices, one of which seemed to have a rear entrance, in the centre of which was the *aedes*, where the standards of the unit would have been kept along with the pay chest. The importance of the building was further underlined by the fact that it was one of the only two within the fort to be surrounded on three sides by stone-lined drains.

The structural focus of the headquarters building is the *aedes*, and a clear line of sight was maintained into it from the main entrance, across the courtyard and through the cross hall, emphasised by the width of the front entrance and the increased spacing between the post holes in the ambulatory and cross hall across this axis. Indeed, the positioning of the headquarters building at the T-junction between the *via principalis* and the *via praetoria* facing the south gate maintains the same focus for the fort as a whole. Such a focus would have been further reinforced by the superstructure of the building, so that the cross hall would have been raised above the height of the front of the building and provided with a clerestory in order to maintain adequate light levels to facilitate the view through to the rear. Such an interpretation is entirely in accord with the size and depth of the post holes and the discontinuous wall trench which define the long sides of the cross hall. If the walls of the *aedes* were raised to the same height as the cross hall, then the structural evidence would indicate that the other offices were also.

Except for the northern range, which abutted the cross hall, the greater depth of the post holes defining the inner wall of the ambulatory compared to the outer wall of the headquarters building suggests that the pitch of the roof sloped away from the central courtyard. This would have a two-fold advantage: it would maximise light levels within the ambulatory and throw rain water out of the building towards the surrounding drains rather than into the central courtyard where there was no provision for carrying it away.

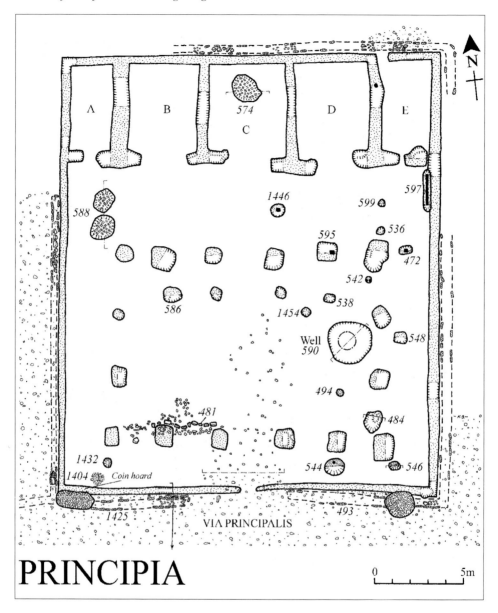

18 Plan of the headquarters building (*principia*)

The second building to be surrounded on three sides by drains was the commanding officer's house or *praetorium* located immediately to the west of the headquarters building and also fronting onto the *via principalis*. It was the largest building in the fort, measuring 28.5m x 23.8m externally, and took the form of a typical Mediterranean peristyle house with four ranges of rooms surrounding a central courtyard (*20*). Again its identification is clear from its position within the fort, its large size, morphology and associated features. The courtyard was clearly the focus of the building. It was

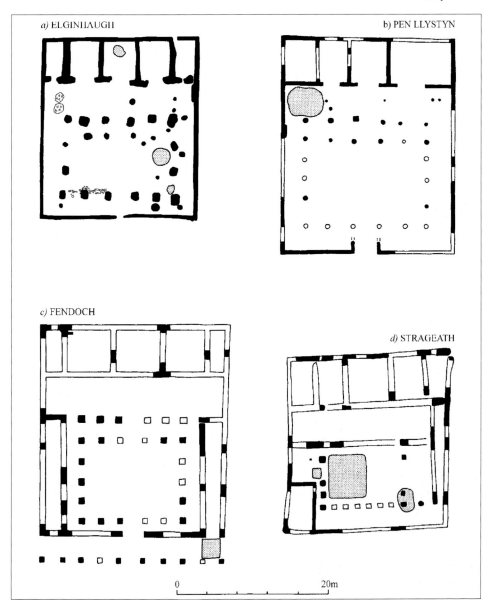

19 Comparative plans of headquarters buildings: a) Elginhaugh; b) Pen Llystyn; c) Fendoch; d) Strageath

large, measuring 18.3m x 11.5m, with a colonnade around its perimeter. This would have provided privacy and seclusion for the commanding officer and his family, as well as ensuring maximum light provision for the surrounding rooms. In the centre was a three-sided rectangular enclosure defined by very slight construction trenches which may have been some form of ornamental feature, such as a low hedge or trellis, perhaps defining a small garden. Only a single main entrance to the building was identified at the front, though parallels suggest that at least one further entrance would have been

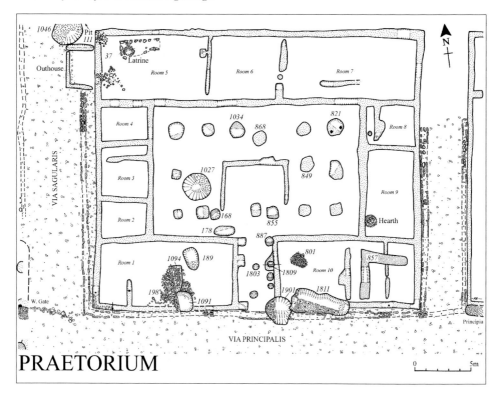

20 Plan of the commanding officer's house (*praetorium*)

provided to allow independent access to the rear range of rooms. The front or southern range comprised two large rooms with various subdivisions on either side of the main entrance passageway, which led through to the courtyard. Room 1 to the west of the passageway may have been the kitchen, since it housed two possible storage pits, whose lower fills contained a few carbonised cereal grains and much charcoal, though the absence of an oven might be taken to undermine this suggestion. A hearth in room 10 on the other side of the passageway looks more likely to have been used for heating than cooking.

The rear portion of the building is likely to have contained the private apartments and the design of the entrance passage, with its multiple doors, implies that there was restricted access beyond the two front rooms (1 and 10). The eastern and western ranges were narrower than either the front or rear ranges and comprised two and three rooms respectively. The largest on the east side (room 9) contained a stone-based hearth. The rear or north range comprised three large rooms, one of which is likely to have served as the dining room, and an attached outhouse or shed. The adjacent room (room 5) contained a stone base or low platform (*colour plate 19*), which incorporated a pit, 0.75m in diameter and 0.3m deep, defined by up to five courses of small sandstone blocks within which were traces of a grey clay lining. A layer of charcoal immediately above the clay lining, derived from the demolition of the fort, suggests that the pit had remained

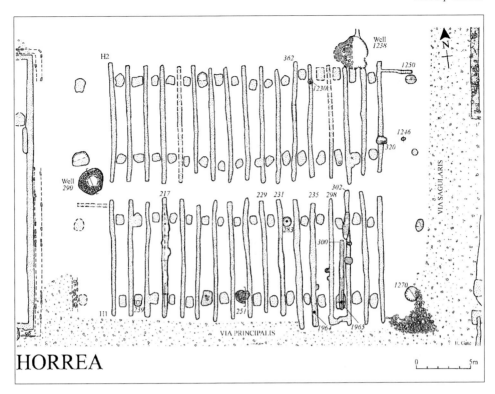

HORREA

21 Plan of the granaries (*horrea*)

open and it seems best interpreted as a private latrine for the commanding officer and his family, though environmental samples taken from the lower fills were unproductive. The outhouse probably marked a rear service access for the latrine, as immediately outside it were three large pits clustered close together. All were steep sided with relatively flat bottoms, their lowest fills consisting of fairly clean sand, and one had been provided with a stone-lined overflow drain, which curved away under the intervallum road to the north-west and fed into the main drain running along the back of the rampart (see *67*), clearly indicating that it had been designed to contain liquid waste.

There is no evidence that any part of the building was other than one storey in height. Each individual range of rooms would have been easily provided with a simple pitched roof, none having a span exceeding 6.0m. The colonnade, which served as an open, but covered, access between rooms, as well as a walkway around the garden, is likely to have been provided with a lean-to roof continuing the roof line of the range against which it was set. The one possible exception is the eastern range, where the double line of posts within the courtyard may indicate a separately covered area, possibly an adaptation to the British climate.

On the other side of the headquarters building were the two granaries (*horrea*), each measuring 24.2 x *c*.9.5m, their entrances facing the east gate to facilitate ready access by wagons. They were readily recognisable by their distinctive plan, made up of seventeen parallel transverse construction trenches creating a network of posts *c.*1.5m apart which would have supported a raised or suspended floor (*21* and *colour plate 11*). This was designed to keep the grain both cool and dry, as well as reduce the possibility of rodent attack. Unusually, however, located between each transverse trench along both sides was a row of posts set in individual post holes, providing further sub-floor support. Each granary had a covered loading bay at each end, which would have made the process of filling and emptying the granary more efficient. Wagons would have been able to back up to the, probably, double doors of the granary and unload directly onto its raised floor under cover.

Because the archaeological remains relate primarily to the sub-floor features, the details of granary superstructures are even more a matter of conjecture than those of other buildings. Accordingly, there have been several suggested reconstructions of Roman timber granaries, including one full-scale, three-dimensional simulation at the Lunt near Coventry (*colour plate 20*). The fundamental question is whether any of the sub-floor posts continued up into the building, for if not, we have no basis for any detailed reconstruction from the archaeological evidence. Indeed, even the width of the building at Elginhaugh is not certain. However, it is likely that two posts would have been needed to support the pitched roof, perhaps in alternate trenches giving a grid of posts to roof height at approximately 3-m centres. There were no roofing tiles recorded from the area of the granary, or indeed from any other part of the fort, so that the roof is likely to have been made up of planks or shingles. Thatch could have been used, but would have provided an ideal refuge for pests. The same objection will no doubt have influenced the choice of material for the infilling of the walls, making the use of wooden cladding more likely than wattle and daub. Indeed, compared to other buildings within the fort, there was a notable absence of burnt daub within the upper levels across the area of the granaries, and the same phenomenon was noted at Usk, Baginton and Crawford. Some form of lean-to roof would have covered the loading bays.

The workshop, or *fabrica*, was a simple rectangular structure measuring 32.2m x 4.2m externally (*22* and *colour plate 14*) set into the rear of the rampart in the north-east corner of the fort opposite the end wall of barracks 3 and 4. Its long and narrow shape was dictated by the space available for, although the rampart had been cut back by 2.7m to accommodate it, the building still projected out into the *via sagularis* reducing the width of that road at the narrowest point to 2.3m. The building was defined on three sides by stone footings that survived to a maximum height of 0.5m with the rampart forming the east side of the building, the roof supported by a line of six apparently irregularly spaced post settings. It was provided with a gravel and cobble floor, which showed signs of extensive areas of burning in places. There were, however, no certainly contemporary internal features. This building is unique within Flavian auxiliary forts in Britain, for the use of stone for construction in this period is confined exclusively to bathhouses, which are located, as at Elginhaugh, outside the fort. Even structures built into or against the rear of the rampart are extremely rare in first-century auxiliary forts, though stone buildings in similar locations are relatively common from the later Antonine period onwards. These parallels would suggest interpretation of the building

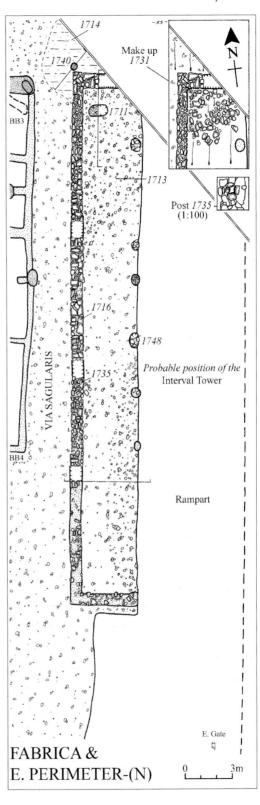

22 Plan of the workshop (*fabrica*) and east
perimeter, northern section

as a bathhouse, but the absence of any of the distinctive features of such a structure and the presence of a bath building outside the fort make this identification highly improbable.

The function of the buildings and the nature of the other activities that are attested around the internal perimeter of forts have one thing in common – the use of fire, either for cooking or metalworking. In the absence of any identifiable cooking oven, particularly in the light of their relative abundance elsewhere in the fort, identification of the building as a workshop, probably for ironworking, seems the most likely. Even though no hammer scale was recovered from any of the levels associated with the workshop, the better preserved deposits at its northern end were clearly iron rich, for the surviving metalling sealed beneath them had been stained orange-brown, presumably as a result of the high concentration of iron oxide in the water leaching through. Given the range and importance of iron artefacts used by the military, from weaponry and tools to nails, the ability at least to repair such items, and probably to manufacture some of them, would seem to be an essential requirement in all forts. This might be considered particularly important in a cavalry fort (see below, chapter four), but for the fact that Roman horses went largely unshod.

The workshop is unlikely to have been more than one-storey high, though for functional reasons it may have had a roof height above the minimum appropriate for barrack blocks. If smithing was taking place within the building, the superstructure may not have been completely enclosed in order both to improve the general ventilation and increase the supply of oxygen to the fire. However, the presence of burnt daub in the plough-disturbed demolition spread that sealed the interior, indicates that above the stone footings much of the west wall would have been in-filled with wattle and daub. A lean-to roof sloping away from the rampart would seem the most sensible arrangement for the purposes of drainage, but the nature of the roofing material is uncertain.

Most of the rest of the fort, both in front (the *praetentura*) and behind (the *retentura*) the central range of buildings, was taken up by stable barracks grouped in pairs. There were some eleven in all, whose identification will be considered in more detail in chapter four. One internal building (building 8) located in the eastern half of the *praetentura* immediately adjacent to the *via praetoria* (*23*) remains to be considered, since it lacked the distinctive internal arrangements of a barrack block. Though structurally paired with barrack 7, onto which it backed, comparison of the relationship of the blocks in the south-east of the fort with those in the south-west, where two pairs of barracks face each other across a narrow road, would suggest that it had a different function. It was of simple rectangular plan measuring *c.*47.4 x 7.6m externally, the latter measurement slightly less than the other barracks. The northern two thirds of the building was subdivided laterally in a manner not unlike that of the *contubernia* partitions in a barrack (below, chapter four), but there was no median longitudinal wall. Four of the rooms were further subdivided along the long axis of the building, but not on the same alignment. The southern third of the building was divided by a single lateral partition into two unequal-sized rooms.

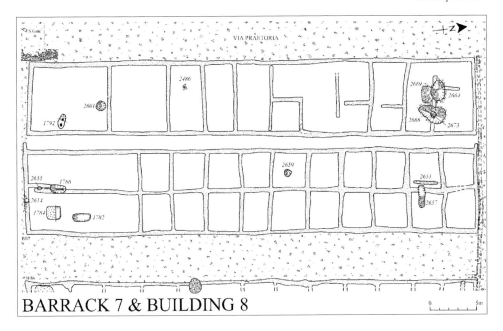

23 Plan of barrack 7 and building 8

Although it superficially resembles a barrack block, all the other barracks in the *praetentura* are so consistent in the details of their layout that any substantial deviations must call this identification into question. Analogies for narrow rectangular buildings in similar locations within auxiliary forts are not far to seek. Two such buildings were identified at Fendoch, one on either side of the *via praetoria*, though these were only 5.5m wide and not investigated in any detail, while at Strageath a building with similar dimensions was located alongside the *via principalis*, though it does at least possess a partial longitudinal partition. But the function of such buildings is rarely asserted with any confidence. The three most commonly suggested interpretations are stable, workshop or storeroom. There is no positive evidence to support its identification as a workshop and an alternative candidate within the fort has better credentials (above). Identification as a stable block is possible, but there is a lack of associated positive evidence and no shortage of accommodation for horses on site (see below, chapter four). Thus, identification of building 8 as some form of storeroom seems the most likely option, though this conclusion is reached on the basis of negative evidence, primarily by a process of elimination, rather than by virtue of any positive attributes, such as an open front to facilitate the entry of wagons or the presence of large quantities of discarded artefacts. A single-storey structure with simple low-pitched roof is assumed, on analogy with the barrack buildings. But there was no median wall to support the ridge and with it much of the weight of the roof, so that the provision of some form of ties across the roof span would have been necessary to prevent the feet of the rafters from causing the wall to spread. The presence of burnt daub and charcoal in demolition contexts at both ends of the building again confirms the use of wattle and daub for the walls.

ORGANISATION AND SUPPLY

The Roman army had no separate engineering corps as is the case in modern armies, but it has been widely assumed that, at least until the second century AD, building skills were largely the prerogative of the legions. For example, in about AD 50 it was legionary detachments that were left behind in Wales to construct garrison posts, and Trajan's Column is both clear and consistent in its depiction of legionary troops engaged in all the building activities that resulted from that emperor's campaigns in Dacia in the early second century (*24*). Where auxiliaries are represented they seem to be standing guard, as might well have been necessary in hostile territory. But it remains uncertain to what extent the hard and fast division of responsibilities depicted on the Column was a reflection of reality. Fragments of auxiliary building inscriptions of Flavian date are known from Cirpi and Aquincum in Pannonia and two daily reports from Vindolanda refer to building activity by the auxiliary garrison in the late Flavian or early Trajanic period, though they seem to relate to repairs or additions to the fort rather than its primary construction. There is no certain direct evidence from Elginhaugh which would indicate whether the fort builders were legionaries or auxiliaries, but at least one and possibly two fragments found during the excavation were from segmental plate armour (*lorica segmentata*), which would normally be associated with legionary troops who were not in garrison (below, chapter four). Accordingly, there may have been a legionary detachment present to build the fort, though any subsequent amendments and repairs were probably undertaken by the auxiliary garrison.

The detailed structural evidence outlined above also provides an indication of the way in which the construction was organised in terms of the general approach, the sequence of the work and the methodology employed. One striking feature of the detailed building plans is their irregularity (see *14*). Though three of the four gateways clearly adhere to the same basic and unusual design, their precise dimensions are all different (compare *9*, *10* and *16*). Similarly, all the barrack blocks in the *praetentura* are broadly the same, but no two are exact replicas of each other (compare *23, 29, 30* and *31*). Moreover, in several of the buildings, most noticeably in barracks 3, 4, 9, 11 and 12, the construction trenches for the main longitudinal walls are sufficiently irregular to make it difficult to maintain a straight wall line through them. The same variability is apparent in the individual structural timbers employed. This is clearest and most evident where the timbers survive or where there was good recovery of post impressions. There is also inconsistency in the species of timber employed. Though oak, the standard building timber in Roman forts, was used occasionally, alder, which is not generally regarded as a timber species suitable for building purposes, is more frequently attested even for the massive structural timbers in the gates and towers.

These variations in structural detail give the strong impression of a rather *ad hoc* approach to the building process. While consistent building designs were being adhered to in general terms, as would be expected in a military organisation, there is no indication of a template or standard plan being employed, nor does the evidence from Elginhaugh support the use of standard, pre-cut, seasoned, structural timbers for any of the buildings,

24 Legionary builders depicted on Trajan's Column

including the gates and towers. In particular, the failure to remove all the bark from several posts and the frequency with which alder was employed in the fort for major structural timbers strongly suggests the use of whatever suitably sized trees were growing locally, or not too far away if the camp at Woodhead, some 7km to the south-west, has been correctly identified as linked to the acquisition of timber for the fort. Indeed, the most common wood remains recovered from waterlogged contexts, other than wells, were off-cuts and splinters from woodworking. These often retained a chord of bark or waney edge, indicating that conversion from round wood was being undertaken on site. The species composition of this assemblage mirrors that of the structural timbers surviving *in situ*, the greatest percentage being of alder with much lesser amounts of oak and hazel, the latter species probably providing most of the wattling.

The evidence does not support the prefabrication on site of whole sections of buildings to allow them to be raised into position as units, as was employed in the famous gate reconstruction at the Lunt in 1970. In principle, the use of post trench rather than sleeper-beam construction is unsuitable for such an approach because of the depth of the foundations into which the units must be placed. Indeed, one reason for the depth of the post trenches is to provide support for free-standing posts during the course of construction. The fact that some posts may have been driven below the bottom of the construction trenches, as evidenced in the commanding officer's house and barrack 10, further confirms their erection as individual elements. It might be

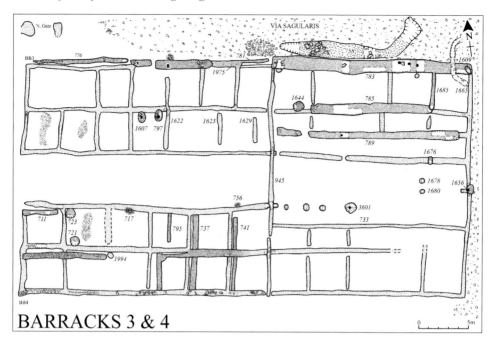

BARRACKS 3 & 4

25 Plan of barracks 3 & 4

thought that the provision of ramps in several post pits in the north, south and east gateways might indicate the erection of prefabricated units, but the different alignments of the ramps, particularly evident at the north gate, demonstrate that they relate to the erection of individual posts, emphasising the difficulty of raising such massive timbers into an upright position individually, let alone in conjoined units of two or three posts.

There are also some clues to the order of the construction work. In several places construction trenches and gate post pits were sealed by road metalling, indicating that the layout of the buildings was established on the ground before the internal roads were constructed. There is also evidence of minor errors in laying out these buildings prior to their erection. In barracks 1 and 7, post trenches projected unnecessarily beyond the outline of the relevant block (see *23* and *27*), while the construction trenches of the end walls of barracks 10 and 11 continued unbroken across the narrow gap between them (see *30*). A more obvious and major example of similar errors is evident in the contemporary fort at Corbridge, Red House, where the alignment of three buildings was changed and the construction trenches of one completely re-dug before any posts had been erected. In all cases except one, the construction trenches in each building at Elginhaugh appear to have been backfilled at the same time. In barracks 3 and 4, however, there were indications of a more piecemeal approach to the construction (*25*). This was particularly noticeable in one of the partition trenches in barrack 3. This cut the median longitudinal trench, which must already have been backfilled. Similarly, the cross wall which marked the western end of the officers' quarters cut three of the main longitudinal wall trenches, two in barrack 4 and one in barrack 3, but was respected by

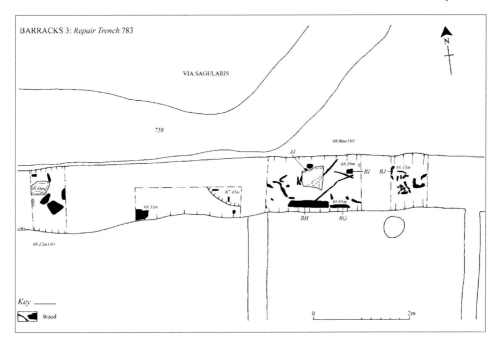

BARRACKS 3: *Repair Trench* 783

VIA SAGULARIS

758

26 Detailed plan of repair trench 783, barrack 3

two others, which stopped short on either side of it. Whether this represents indecision about the precise nature of the building, delay during its construction, or simply a lack of discipline in the process, cannot be determined.

REBUILDING, REPAIR AND MAINTENANCE

Finally, it is worth noting that, despite the relatively short period of occupation of the fort, several of the buildings appear to have required repairs or minor modification. In the headquarters building, the provision of additional posts in the ambulatory and cross hall seems to indicate the need for extra roof supports (see *18*). Room 10 at the front of the commanding officer's house had been modified with the insertion of a very wide L-shaped construction trench amending the previous room divisions and additional support was provided on the eastern wall of the entrance passage, and perhaps in the veranda in the central courtyard (see *20*). One of the outer post holes was re-cut and new transverse slot inserted towards the front of granary 1 (*21*). Since the slot falls short of the postulated position of the walls of the granary at both ends, it seems likely that the repair was achieved simply by removing the floor to insert new posts or to replace old ones without affecting the rest of the superstructure.

The interior subdivisions in several of the barracks were modified, the significance of which will be discussed in chapter four. In addition, a number of the barracks showed some signs of small-scale repairs. Additional posts were provided to prop up the western end walls of barracks 1 and 2, the former involving first a single post set in a deep pit which was itself then replaced by three posts in a shallower pit filled with cobbles and angular stones (see *27*). In all cases, these repair posts seem to have been considerably larger than those in the original construction. The longitudinal central wall trenches in barracks 5 and 7 were partly widened or supplemented, mainly at the officers' end of the block. These repairs were generally quite minor and may reflect the use of less suitable structural timbers, such as alder, whose resistance to rot is considerably less than oak. In the case of barrack 3 and 4, however, the repairs were considerably more substantial and of more than one phase, involving the complete replacement of load-bearing walls by new ones set in foundations of massive size (*25, 26*). The survival of structural timbers in these trenches, both *in situ* and discarded, serves to indicate that excessive dampness was the problem, presumably caused by a combination of the poorly draining clay-silt subsoil and the fact that, because of the topography, rain water from much of the northern part of the fort drained down into the north-east corner. In such circumstances, the stability of the structure is likely to have been threatened and the need for repair an on-going problem.

Some five posts in the south gate, four in the west tower and one in the east, all situated towards the front of the gateway, were replaced (see *16*). This seems more likely to have occurred as a single event rather than the posts being replaced piecemeal because of the juxtaposition of most of the posts involved and the careful re-cutting of the primary post pits in order to maintain as far as possible the original position of the uprights. Individual repairs would have been more easily achieved simply by inserting a new post alongside the one that was beginning to fail. Since there is no indication that the gate was blocked and then recommissioned, as in the case of both the east and west gates (below, chapter seven), it is assumed that these changes represent a repair or major overhaul during the life of the fort. In addition, the central pit of the gate portal was cut into by a smaller post pit too shallow to be a replacement, so best interpreted as some form of additional support for the superstructure.

Finally, there were slight signs of repairs or alterations to some of the buildings in the annexe, particularly A and G, despite their even shorter life than those within the fort (see below, chapter five). One or two post holes cut wall construction trenches, while others were dug close up against them, suggesting that additional support was required. In one case, in building A, a localised secondary thickening of the construction trench indicated replacement of a slightly larger section of walling.

FOUR

INFANTRY OR CAVALRY?

It has long been axiomatic in Roman military studies that there is some direct and, therefore, recoverable connection between the plan of an auxiliary fort and the type of unit in garrison. Moreover, it has also been widely accepted that it was the norm for the different types of auxiliary unit to be separately housed in their own custom built forts. A simple correlation between fort and garrison, based primarily on internal area and barrack provision, was originally put forward by Sir Ian Richmond in the mid-1950s and continued to be refined and reviewed up to the early 80s.

Increasingly since that time, however, this assumed correlation has been seriously challenged as Roman military archaeologists have failed to establish any consistent relationship between attested primary garrison and fort size, despite the increased level of data recovery. This has led to the suggestion that some forts must have contained composite garrisons. Certainly, there is no shortage of papyrological evidence indicating that detachments were often split from larger units to operate independently on a semi-permanent basis. In one famous example relating to *cohors XX Palmyrenorum milliaria equitata* (the twentieth-part mounted cohort of Palmyrenes, 1000 strong) stationed at Dura Europos in Syria in the early third century AD, duty rosters for two different years indicate, not only that the strength of each century of infantry and squadron (*turma*) of cavalry varied considerably from the theoretical norm (see below), but that up to a fifth of the unit was serving away from Dura. Closer to Elginhaugh, both chronologically and geographically, elucidation of an imperial duty roster of *c.*AD 90 from Vindolanda in Northumberland confirms that some 50 per cent of the unit was stationed at Corbridge, 13 miles away to the east. Since a smaller group was absent elsewhere on other duties, this left only 45 per cent of the unit at Vindolanda, though there are also suggestions that parts of two or more units may have been brigaded together at the site. It has become increasingly evident, and is now more widely accepted, that forts constructed for single units were the exception rather the rule. Indeed, it has become difficult to reconcile the number of auxiliary units known with the increasing number of forts attested in the Flavian period in north Britain.

New discoveries from the air in recent decades include Blennerhasset in Cumbria and Ladyward in Dumfries and Galloway and it is clear, on grounds of topography and logical strategic dispositions, that many more remain to be discovered, as for example at the crossing of the Tweed and in south-west Scotland. Yet the number of Flavian auxiliary forts currently known in north Britain already exceeds by over 50 per cent the number of units attested in the army of the province at the time, as understood from epigraphic and historical sources. While it is possible that the size of the army was considerably larger than these sources attest, this grows increasingly improbable as the number of forts continues to increase. It has already been argued that Flavian forts in Wales and northern England may have been abandoned in order to pursue the conquest of Scotland. But it may well be that the occupation of auxiliary forts was much more fluid and flexible than has previously been assumed and it is becoming increasingly apparent that fort garrisons need not correspond with full auxiliary units. We should not necessarily expect, therefore, that the barrack accommodation in any auxiliary fort would neatly fit the hypothetical or paper strength of any designated unit.

The auxiliaries were non-citizen troops recruited on a tribal or provincial basis and posted usually some distance from their homeland to serve Rome. They were formed into three types of unit – *alae* or wings of cavalry, cohorts of infantry and *cohortes equitatae* (mounted cohorts) which combined both infantry and cavalry; each of which could be either 500 (*quingenaria*) or nominally 1000 (*milliaria*) strong, though the smaller units were much more common. The infantry were divided into centuries under the command of a centurion and the cavalry into *turmae* or squadrons under the command of a decurion, and each century or *turma* further subdivided into *contubernia* or tent parties – the group of men who shared a tent on campaign or a subdivision of a barrack block in a permanent fort. Though the size of these various units and their component parts is broadly understood, it is not necessarily definitively established in all cases, particularly in relation to any cavalry element. While the size of an infantry century and the number of men per *contubernium* is generally agreed as eighty and eight respectively, based primarily on the author Hyginus, who wrote a treatise on castramentation, there is considerably more debate about the size of a cavalry *turma*. The traditional figure is 32, based on that for legionary cavalry referred to in the fourth-century military manual by Vegetius and supported by dividing the overall figure for an *ala quingenaria* (512), provided by Arrian in his second-century AD treatise on military tactics, by the number of *turmae* (16) in that unit attested by Hyginus and confirmed in a late first-century ink writing tablet from Carlisle which lists the issue of wheat and barley to the *turmae* of an *ala* stationed in the fort there. But estimates ranging from 24 to 70 have been variously proposed, based primarily on attempts to reconcile disparate papyrological evidence with varying barrack plans.

A further major area of contention has been the manner in which horses were stabled and, accordingly, the very identification of the presence of cavalry within forts. Some buildings in auxiliary forts have been tentatively identified as stables in the past, either because they were provided with some form of additional drainage facilities, or because the number of barracks known exceeded the necessary provision for the unit assumed to have been in garrison, or simply because cavalry were attested and, therefore, stables were required. However, given the number of auxiliary forts that have been examined across the Empire, examples of stables which can be identified with certainty have proved to be exceedingly rare. This is all the more surprising when cavalry units,

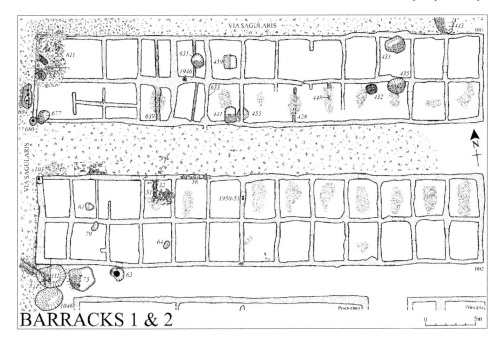

27 Plan of barracks 1 & 2

whether *alae* or *cohortes equitatae*, were by far the most common auxiliary units in the Roman army, representing some 74 per cent of the units attested in Britain in the mid-second century. One possibility put forward by way of explanation of this deficiency is that the horses would have been kept outside, either on grazing land or in an annexe, rather than confined in stables. There is some limited evidence for this too in the annexe at Elginhaugh (below, chapter five), where a possible picket line for horses may be the explanation for a rail fence in an otherwise open space. More recently, however, a more radical explanation has been put forward (see below).

Given these difficulties, rather than attempting to identify a specific single unit type at Elginhaugh on the basis of its best fit with the barrack accommodation attested, the size of the garrison and whether or not cavalry troops were present has been estimated from first principles for each accommodation block. With that said, this in turn may lead to a possible identification of the unit type or types involved.

Two forms of barrack block are represented at Elginhaugh. The first, of which nine examples are present, is a simple rectangular block some 8.3-8.5m wide and between 44.4m and 47.6m long, the shorter examples reflecting the lesser space available in the *retentura* where the blocks were arranged across the width of the fort (*27*). The barracks were generally laid out in pairs. Barracks 1 and 2 faced each other across a *c.*5m wide metalled road, as did barracks 9 and 10, 11 and 12, and 6 and 7 (see *14*). Building 8 disrupted the pattern in the south-east quadrant of the fort, so that this left barrack 5 to stand alone backing onto the *via sagularis* and facing the back of barrack 6 across a much narrower metalled road some 3.2m wide.

Each block was divided centrally and subdivided laterally into ten sets of equal-sized double rooms, the *contubernia*. The quarters for the officers are clearly distinguished by the provision of additional and irregular subdivisions and other features, and took up the outer 10-12m nearest to the rampart, representing some 22.5-25.2 per cent of each block. On generally accepted assumptions about the number of men per *contubernium* noted above, these blocks at first appeared to represent infantry barracks for a century of eighty men with the centurion's quarters at the end nearest to the rampart. The proportion of the block given over to the officer's quarters also fits neatly into the norm for infantry barrack blocks, though in the Flavian period barracks with wider officer's quarters and verandahs are slightly more common than the simple rectangular form attested at Elginhaugh. Closest parallels are provided at Pen Llystyn and Strageath (*28*), though in both of those cases the blocks are found in combination with the more common L-shaped type.

However, the presence of unusual amorphous orange-red stains was noted in several of the blocks, whose significance was puzzling and not readily paralleled. They were first identified in barracks 1 and 2 where they were approximately centrally located in the front room of almost every *contubernium*, and in the rear room also in at least one example in barrack 2 (*27* and *colour plate 3*). The features tended to be longer than they were broad with their long axis aligned north–south across the length of the room. Several examples were positioned slightly more towards one side of the room. Where this phenomenon was apparent, the shift was consistent within each block, but different between the two; towards the eastern end of barrack 1 and the western end of barrack 2. The texture of the soil was consistent both within and beyond the areas of staining and there was no sign of any associated cut, so they do not represent the infilling of any feature penetrating the subsoil. They ranged in size from as little as 1.5m x 0.6m to 3.6m x 1.4m, penetrating to a maximum depth of 0.2m where sampled. The core of each stain was red-brown, shading to orange towards the edges, but there were no traces of burning, neither charcoal, ash nor burnt daub.

Two hypotheses were considered during the excavation: that the stains in the subsoil were caused by the differential oxidation of the minerals within the sandy subsoil as a result of indirect heat emanating from centrally located hearths or braziers, or that they were created by a chemical reaction to the passage through the soil of horse urine. Accordingly, samples for both chemical and magnetic analysis were extracted. The results, however, proved inconclusive, though it was noted that the reddening did not resemble that due to burning as much as that due to the precipitation of Iron III compounds and no positive response was obtained to tests for remanent magnetism as might have been expected if they resulted from sustained heating of the subsoil.

The provision of heating within *contubernia* is common, though hearths are more frequently attested from excavations in Germany than in Britain. However, they are usually found set against the central partition wall in the sleeping room (*papilio*) at the rear, though they are occasionally attested in a variety of other locations, including the middle of the front room, which is usually regarded as the place where equipment and personal possessions were stored and generally referred to as the *arma*. A single secondary

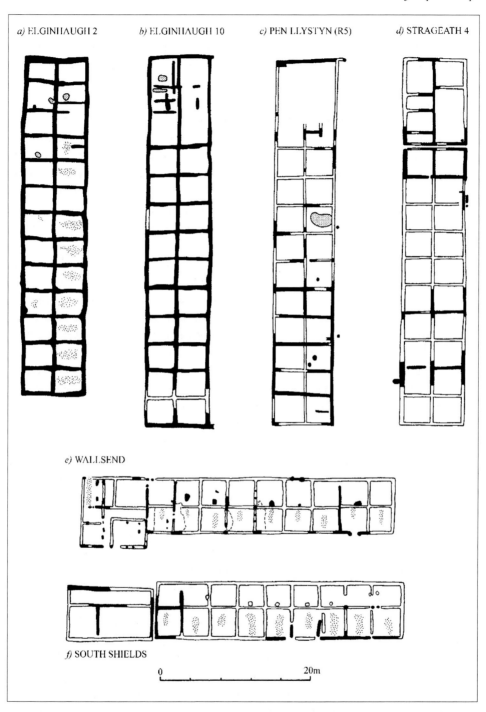

a) ELGINHAUGH 2   b) ELGINHAUGH 10   c) PEN LLYSTYN (R5)   d) STRAGEATH 4

e) WALLSEND

f) SOUTH SHIELDS

0   20m

28 Comparative barrack plans: a) Elginhaugh (2); b) Elginhaugh (10); c) Pen Llystyn; d) Strageath;
e) Wallsend; f) South Shields

hearth is attested at Elginhaugh in one *contubernium* in barrack 1 situated towards the rear of the *arma*. That it should survive, while no hearths from phase 1 did so, is presumably a reflection of its construction in stone and concomitant greater visibility during excavation. However, the much smaller size of the hearth and the limited discolouration of the soil around it make it less likely that the more widespread staining from the earlier phase was the result of internal heating arrangements, unless very sizeable moveable braziers had been employed. Nonetheless, in the early stages of the post-excavation analysis of the fort this seemed to be the best solution, since if all the blocks where these stains were attested were interpreted as separate stables, there would not have been sufficient barrack accommodation for the men.

The best analogies for the stains, however, at least in terms of surface dimensions and location, are provided by shallow pits or scoops which were originally identified in two barrack blocks at Dormagen in Germany, where environmental and chemical evidence, specifically the recovery of hay and horse fodder in the pits and the higher phosphate levels around them, confirmed that they did relate to the stabling of horses. Subsequently, Sebastian Sommer examined further examples of such soakaway pits at Ladenburg identifying what he called 'Stallbaracken' (stable barracks) there and postulating other examples at a number of sites in Germany, arguing that horses and men would have been commonly accommodated together. Most recently, stable barracks have been extensively excavated at two sites at the western end of Hadrian's Wall, Wallsend and South Shields, and further possible examples from Britain and the Danube frontier assembled by Nick Hodgson (*28*). It was this work which provided a solution, for it removed the need to assume that blocks had to be either stables or barracks, recognising that the combination of the two functions in one building should increasingly be seen as the norm. This raises the possibility that many more so-called barracks may in fact have been stable barracks.

The one crucial difference between all the site evidence assembled by Sebastian Sommer and Nick Hodgson and that from Elginhaugh, however, is the absence of any associated soakaway pit or scoop at the latter. With that said, the preservation of shallow cut features across much of the site was poor. This was the result of either severe plough truncation, particularly evident across barracks 1 and 2, or the general difficulty of identifying cuts at higher levels within the soil profile and the subsequent removal by machine of the worm-sorted upper soil horizon at an early stage in the excavation (chapter one). Given the number of stable barracks that have now been positively identified in the north-western provinces of the Empire, the probability is high that these amorphous areas of soil discolouration in the centre of the front room of each *contubernium* of barracks 1 and 2 do indeed represent staining from animal urine penetrating beneath shallow pits or scoops which themselves have not survived, particularly as the soakaway pits recorded in the stable barracks at Wallsend were quite shallow, ranging from 0.18-0.4m in depth.

Unfortunately, the frequency of the identification of these areas of staining was not consistent across the fort at Elginhaugh. In only three of the nine simple rectangular barrack blocks (1, 2 and 5) (*27, 29*) were they sufficiently regular to assert with confidence that they were a standard provision, and only in the latter were they also attested in the

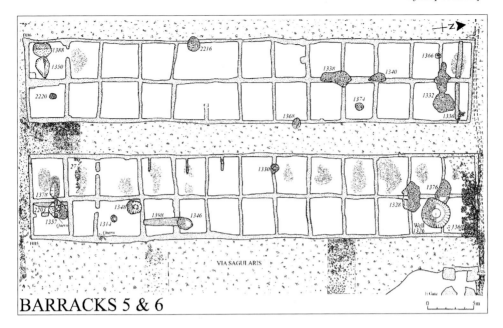

29 Plan of barracks 5 & 6

officers' quarters. In two other barracks (6 and 9) (*29, 30*) only one or two orange-red stains were attested, though including one in the officers' quarters in both cases. Failure to identify more may have been caused by local differences in the subsoil, for it was noticeable that the stains were most readily recognisable in those areas of the site where the subsoil was predominantly sandy. There were sufficient examples, however, to assert that these blocks too were likely to have housed cavalry.

Those barrack blocks (nos 7, and 10-12) (*23, 30, 31*), where no stains from soakaway pits are attested, may be infantry barracks, but their location coincides largely with areas of the fort constructed on damper subsoil and this may have affected the potential visibility of these chemically-induced stains. There are other hints, however, that the same functional identification may apply. In the case of barrack 7, a demolition pit (1784) included in its fill large quantities of carbonised barley and some straw, which may derive from animal feed and bedding, though it could simply represent material which had spread from the adjacent blocks during demolition. Although there is no grain from demolition contexts across barracks 10-12 which is identifiable to species, there are a few grains of barley from pit 1565 in barrack 10 and quantities of cereals, including both barley and wheat, from the ovens adjacent to barracks 11 and 12 (chapter six). It cannot be asserted with complete confidence, therefore, that blocks 7 and 10-12 were not also stable barracks.

Further support for the housing of horses within the fort is provided by some of the artefactual evidence. Several copper alloy harness fittings were recovered from the site (*32*), including part of single-link bridle from the topsoil; a fragment of a terret from the demolition fill of large pit behind the east-south-east interval tower (no. 16); two

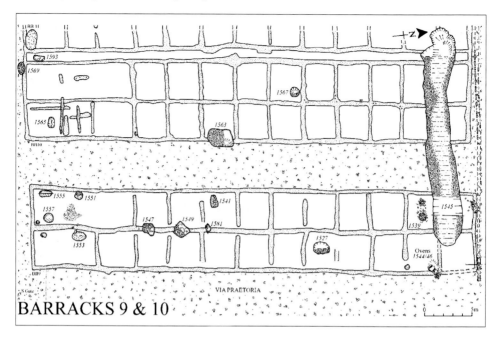

30 Plan of barracks 9 & 10

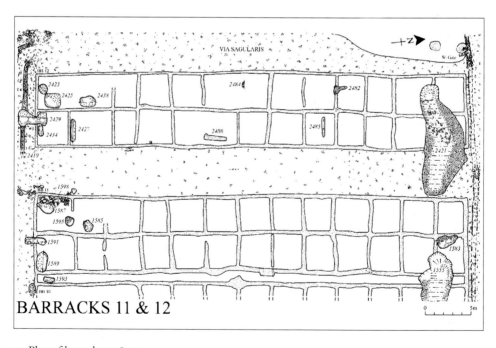

31 Plan of barracks 11 & 12

button-and-loop fasteners, one from post-Roman plough soil (no. 17), the other from the fill of the annexe enclosing ditch; one crescentic (no. 19) and one circular (no. 20) decorated harness mount from the primary fill of the inner fort ditch and from post-Roman plough soil respectively; and two junction loops from harness, one from the upper demolition fill of pit 75 between *praetorium* and barrack 2 (no. 21) and the other from post-Roman plough soil. Similarly, the relatively large number of glass and faience melon beads from the site may be taken as a further indicator of a cavalry presence, since they are often found in some quantity at military sites and seem to have some association with cavalry. Though interpretation of their function is not certain, larger examples would have been very cumbersome in a necklace and it possible that some were worn by horses or used as decorative elements on horse harness, like the beads portrayed on a decorative strap around the neck of a horse on a tombstone from Cologne. Many of the beads show signs of heavy wear at their perforations caused by them being constantly rubbed against each other, such as by the movement of a horse. Over thirty were recovered from various locations around the fort, including from metalling at the front entrance of the headquarters building, from pits in the commanding officer's house and barrack 1, 11 and 12 and from general demolition spreads over barracks 5, 6, 9 and 12.

In addition, the fact that relatively large numbers of animals were present within the fort is supported by the generally high frequency of charred barley and oat grains recovered (66.5 per cent and 4.2 per cent respectively), cereals which were predominantly for animal consumption, compared to wheat for the troops (29.2 per cent). These percentages contrast markedly with those for the annexe, where the ratios are effectively reversed. More specifically, pits 439 and 435 in barrack 1 both contained quantities of carbonised barley, while the latter also contained oats and some straw, possibly derived from animal feed and bedding. The presence of large quantities of barley and some straw in demolition pits in two of the barracks (1 and 5) adds further weight to the argument that they were, indeed, stable barracks.

Thus, the evidence for the predominance of cavalry within the fort seems undeniable. To complicate matters further, however, an entirely different type of barrack is represented by two conjoined structures, barracks 3 and 4 (see 25). The overall length of the block and width of the men's accommodation is the same as the other two barracks in the *retentura* (barracks 1 and 2) and the identification of orange-red stains in three of the *contubernia* again indicates the presence of horses. But the similarities end there. Only six or seven *contubernia* are in evidence and the officers' quarters are quite massive in comparison to the other barracks (*Table 1*), since they occupy not only a greater proportion of the length of each block, but also the gap between them. Even allowing for the possibility that more than one officer would have been in residence, and so dividing the area by two, this still represents a space provision more than double that in the other barracks in the fort. Indeed, the full provision is up to twice that provided for a legionary centurion at Inchtuthil. This raises the strong possibility that stable barracks 3/4 accommodated troops whose status was higher than that of troops elsewhere in the fort.

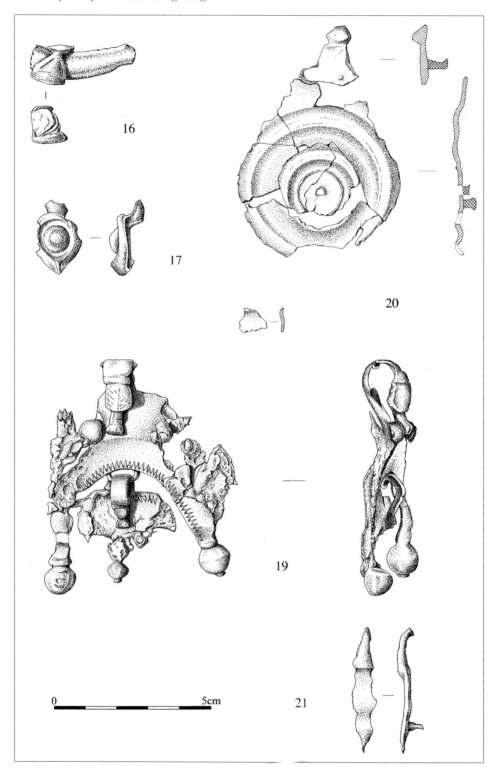

32 Copper alloy harness fittings (nos 16-21)

Table 1 Barrack dimensions at Elginhaugh compared to Strageath and Inchtuthil

Barracks	Overalllength	Width of mens' quarters	Officers' quarters length	Internal area
Elginhaugh 1-2	44.4m	8.4m (8.35m-8.75m)	10m	84m²
Elginhaugh 3/4	44.3m	8.4m	19.7m	437m²★
Elginhaugh 5-7	47.6m	8.5m	12m	102m²
Elginhaugh 9-10	47.3m	8.3m	11.2m-11.8m	93-98m²
Elginhaugh 11-12	47.2m	8.1m (7.8m-8.4m)	11.3m-11.9m	91.5-96m²
Strageath I	47.85m	8.5m	19.5m	217m²
Inchtuthil	83.8m	7.9-8.5m	20.1-22.25m	214-246m²

★ This is the combined figure for the double block

There are at least four plausible explanations for the large size of the officers' quarters in barracks 3 and 4. Perhaps the simplest is that the block contained elements of two *turmae* of cavalry, as its split layout might suggest, and so the officers' quarters had to accommodate two decurions and accompanying under officers (*principales*). Even so, dividing the officers' quarters into two still gives an area considerably larger than the norm. Alternatively, it might have housed the senior decurion (*decurio princeps*), whose existence is attested epigraphically, if infrequently, providing him with enhanced accommodation as a reflection of his superior status. Thirdly, the larger size of officers' quarters might be explained if the garrison had been made up of elements from different units, including *turmae* from both an *ala quingenaria* and a *cohors quingenaria equitata*, the former occupying stable barracks 3 and 4 since they were of higher status. Were such large officers' quarters the norm for an *ala*, however, it might be expected that they would be much more commonly recorded than they are, unless the troops had come from an *ala milliaria*, a much rarer unit type which first appears in the mid-Flavian period whose *turmae*, some commentators suggest, were also larger in size.

A fourth possibility which must be considered, is that barracks 3 and 4 provided accommodation for a legionary century. This was the explanation favoured by Sheppard Frere and John Wilkes to explain the large size of the officer's quarters in barrack I at Strageath. Two finds of military equipment might be taken to provide support for a legionary presence at Elginhaugh. Firstly, there are the two separate catapult elements recovered from the site (below, chapter six), since artillery is normally considered the preserve of the legions. However, it is clear that at least one of these pieces, the washer, comes from a small hand-held weapon and the association of such 'little catapults' with auxiliary forces is now recognised as unproblematic. Secondly, the limited amount of discarded armour amongst the finds from Elginhaugh includes at least one and possibly two pieces of segmental plate armour (*lorica segmentata*), which again would normally be associated with legionary troops. But such finds are surprisingly common in auxiliary forts and there has been considerable debate about their likely significance. At one extreme they have been taken to indicate a legionary garrison, while at the other it has been argued that a clear-cut distinction between legionary and auxiliary armour should no longer be assumed. The debate remains unresolved. Recent discussions of the evidence for legionary armour have concluded that the wearing of *lorica segmentata* by auxiliaries cannot be substantiated. But neither, on the other hand, can the presence of small numbers of legionary troops in numerous auxiliary forts be sustained, either logically as a sensible disposition of limited specialist forces, or archaeologically in terms of attested barrack accommodation. Though barracks 3 and 4 together have sufficient *contubernia* of adequate size to house a century of legionary troops, the officers' quarters are actually too large for a single centurion, being approximately twice the size of the average centurion's quarters in the contemporary barracks at Inchtuthil (*Table 1*). More telling, however, since legionaries were the infantry troops *par exellence*, are the stains from soakaways in three of the *contubernia*, which attest the presence of horses. On present evidence, therefore, the *lorica segmentata* fragments seem best interpreted as lost, or broken and discarded, by legionary troops either during the construction of the fort or possibly, given the context of one in the backfilling of the grain drier (chapter five), while a detachment was temporarily working in the annexe.

The final piece of evidence which lends further general support to the suggestion of a predominantly higher status cavalry contingent within the fort is the size of the bathhouse (below, chapter six) (see *2* and *64*). Very few Flavian bathhouses have been identified to provide comparators, but the Elginhaugh example was considerably larger than the average auxiliary fort baths built in the Antonine period. Indeed, in terms of internal floor space, excluding the area occupied by the plunge baths, the Elginhaugh baths are no less spacious than those at contemporary Newstead, a much larger fort perhaps with a legionary presence, and half as big again as the legionary bath suite at Inchtuthil, though the latter was probably intended only for the officers, the main internal baths never having been built.

Having determined that most, possibly all of the accommodation blocks at Elginhaugh were stable barracks, we must return to the issue of how many troops and how many horses would have been accommodated in each block. With the exception of one internal wall in the officers' quarters in barrack 1, there were no gaps in the wall trenches to indicate the location of doorways into the *contubernia*. However, the size and location of the subsoil stains from soakaway pits is instructive. Given the intended function of the pits to collect urine, that they were aligned across the length of the room indicates that the horses must have been tethered to one of the side walls of the *contubernia*. The tendency of the pits to be located slightly off centre in each *contubernium* further suggests that the horses would have had their heads against the side furthest from the pits, leaving space behind their hindquarters for a walkway from the front entrance to the rear accommodation for the troopers. In most cases, the stable barracks faced each other in pairs, so that this configuration would have resulted in the horses in the two opposing barracks facing in opposite directions, so that the doorways to the *contubernia* would not have been directly opposite each other, a sensible arrangement if horses were to be led in or out of the two blocks at the same time. With their heads against one of the side walls of a *contubernium*, the room depth of 4.1m would provide ample space for three horses to be tethered side by side. Though this would allow slightly less than the 1.52m per horse recommended by a British War Office manual of 1904 for horse lines, it is clear that the horses used by the Roman military were smaller than modern examples, averaging less than 14 hands (1.42m) compared to some 16 hands (1.63m) to the withers. Indeed, the space available is slightly in excess of that in the timber phase stable barracks at Wallsend. On the basis of the reconstruction postulated there by Nick Hodgson and Paul Bidwell, each *contubernium* would then have accommodated three troopers in the rear room with their horses at the front. Accordingly, each stable barrack at Elginhaugh with its ten *contubernia* would have housed a *turma* of thirty cavalrymen. The three examples of soakaways attested in the officers' quarters in barrack 5, which are of equivalent dimensions to those in the men's quarters (see *29*), would indicate facilities sufficient for up to nine horses, which adds support to the suggestion that the decurion would have shared his accommodation with two under officers (*principales*) along with their remounts, since according to Hyginus in his treatise on castramentation, the decurion had three horses and the *principales* two. This would give a *turma* strength of 31-33, very close to the traditionally accepted figure noted above.

In the absence of epigraphic or papyrological evidence, the type or types of unit involved at Elginhaugh cannot be determined with certainty. However, if the assumptions about the size of centuries and *turmae* and the numbers of men per *contubernium* are correct, and the identifications of stable barracks listed in *Table 2* below are justified, this would indicate a possible garrison of six *turmae* of cavalry, one of which in barracks 3 and 4 is slightly larger, and four centuries of infantry – assuming all the composite elements were at full strength, that would give a garrison of 509, excluding the officers. Including them would add a further 11-29 men, depending upon how many were sharing the officers' accommodation. If, however, the four barracks, which provided no evidence of soakaways, were also stable barracks, as may well have been the case, that would give a garrison of ten *turmae* of cavalry, again with one slightly enlarged, totalling 309 men, excluding the officers. Including the decurions and under officers housed in the officers' quarters, would increase the figure to 342. Neither configuration corresponds with any standard unit. If the garrison represents part of a single unit, it is most likely to derive from an *ala quingenaria*, since there are too many *turmae* for a *cohors quingenaria equitata* and milliary units are relatively rare. This is perhaps the simplest solution and, therefore, the one favoured here.

Such a conclusion finds tentative support elsewhere. At least one phase of the fort at Carlisle appears to have housed the *ala Gallorum Sebosiana* under the governorship of Agricola, since both are mentioned on a fragmentary writing tablet recovered from a later pit on the site. On the basis of the presence at Carlisle of stamped mortaria made at Elginhaugh, it has been suggested by Vivien Swan that this 500-strong cavalry unit may have been split between Elginhaugh and possibly Newstead before being reunited at Carlisle, though none of the dendrochronologically-dated phases of construction there (AD 72/3; 83/4 and 93/4) quite match the date of abandonment of Elginhaugh.

Table 2 Location of urine soakaways and barrack identification at Elginhaugh

Barracks	Soakaways in Men's quarters	Soakaways in Officers' quarters	Identification
1–2	9	none	stable barracks
3–4	2/1	none	stable barracks
5	8	3	stable barracks
6	1	1	stable barracks
7	none	none	barracks or possible stable barracks
9	none	1	stable barracks
10	none	none	barracks or possible stable barracks
11–12	none	none	barracks or possible stable barracks

Finally, there were clear traces of a second structural phase in most of the barracks, involving the remodelling of the men's accommodation. Clearly this must have implications for the size of the garrison, but the evidence is only fragmentary so that it is difficult to establish the full picture. Refurbishment of the barracks, involving the moving of the transverse walls which defined the *contubernia*, was identified in barracks 1-6 and 12. The best surviving evidence came from barrack 1, where the remodelling seems to have resulted in a slight increase in the size of the officers' quarters to 26 per cent of the total, though only to the extent that it was brought into line with those barracks in the *praetentura* (see *27*). More significant, however, was the suggestion of a reduction in the accommodation for the troops. Four of the primary *contubernia* were bisected by walls running across the width of the building. These subdivisions were clearly secondary, for in three cases they cut through the amorphous orange-red stains in the centre of the primary *contubernia* and were probably the surviving remains of a complete recasting of the interior of the barrack which would have reduced the number of *contubernia* to nine or eight. Such secondary subdivisions are likely to have been based on shallower construction trenches than primary ones, and hence their poorer survival in an area of heavy plough truncation and the failure to recover the full complement. There was one hint of a similar reorganisation in barrack 2 where in one *contubernium* adjacent to the officers' quarters a construction trench overlay the remains of one of the amorphous orange-red stains. Though the pattern elsewhere was less clear-cut, the general impression gained is of a slight reduction in the number of *contubernia*. A subsidiary partition slot through the centre of the front room towards the middle of the men's quarters in barrack 4 may hint at a similar remodelling of the interior, but the traces were difficult to disentangle from the abundant evidence of extensive repairs. Slight traces of additional partition slots were recorded extending up to 1.5m from the west wall of barrack 5 and in two cases these slots cut the urine soakaway stains in the centre of the front room (see *29*), though their relationship with the outer wall was not confirmed by excavation. Even less survived in barrack 6, where two slots on the same east–west alignment inserted towards the middle of the first *contubernium* effectively reduced the length of the block by 1.3m. Again, the front example cut through the remains of a urine soakaway stain and clearly cut both the median and outer longitudinal wall trenches.

The remodelled barracks appear not to have been provided with soakaways for horse urine. This may suggest a change in garrison from a cavalry *turma* to an infantry cohort, the latter presumably with a slightly reduced strength, the larger officer's quarters reflecting the higher rank of the centurion compared to the decurion, but such an interpretation may be placing too much emphasis on relatively slight and poorly preserved changes to the accommodation and the failure to recover the slight remains of any potentially associated shallow urine pits. In this context it should be noted that the first phase stable barracks at Wallsend had only nine *contubernia*, interpreted by Nick Hodgson as indicating a *turma* strength of only 30. The implications for the size and nature of the garrison can, then, only be tentative, but the alterations do not seem to be sufficiently drastic to warrant the suggestion of a significant change of garrison, particularly as they were not mirrored in the central range, and may reflect recognition of the actual rather than the paper strength of the original garrison with a concomitant increase in space provision for those remaining in residence. Even if each of the barracks involved effectively lost one *contubernium*, assuming that the garrison has been correctly identified as cavalry and continued to be so, this would have resulted in a reduction in the potential total garrison of less than 25 men.

FIVE

SOLDIER OR CIVILIAN?

CHARACTER OF THE ANNEXE

Attached enclosures, usually referred to as annexes, are a common feature of Roman auxiliary forts and fortlets in north and west Britain. Indeed, multiple annexes are not infrequently attested (see below). Though their size, location and relationship with forts has been briefly analysed, few consistent patterns have emerged. Annexes vary considerably in area and are found at all points of the compass relative to their associated fort. They commonly extend across the whole of one side of the fort, as at Elginhaugh where the annexe was located along its west side (*1* and *3*). Though the full extent of the annexe could not be determined, since its western limit lay beyond the field available for examination, the total area enclosed was at least 6 acres (2.5ha), some 50 per cent larger than the fort. This is a less common feature, though notable examples in Scotland would include Ardoch, Duntocher, Rough Castle and Oxton, most of which are of later, Antonine date.

The annexe was defined by only a single ditch. This was relatively narrow (*c*.1.5m) and shallow (0.8m) with a V-shaped profile on the south side, but generally larger, though more variable, in its dimensions on the north side, up to from 5.2m in width and 1.4m deep, with a gently sloping outer face and a more sharply defined inner one (*33*). It is possible that these increased dimensions derive from a re-cutting of the ditch. No traces survived of a rampart inside the annexe ditch, though presumably one existed. The only positive evidence was a shallow, almost flat-bottomed gully running approximately parallel with and some 0.6-1.0m to the rear of the ditch, detected in trench 6 on the north side which may represent support for some form of revetment or fence line (*33* and *34*).

The line of the ditch on the south side appears to follow a logical course along the edge of the flat plateau on which the fort stands, presumably joining the fort ditches at their south-west corner. The line of the ditch on the north side is less easily determined or explained. It did not join the fort ditches at the north-west corner as anticipated, but probably continued, more or less in a straight line, to join the outer ditch of the fort, assuming that, as on the east and west sides, it had four. Unfortunately there was no time available to follow the line, once it had been established by extending the original trench to the north. By this time the probable point of intersection had been covered

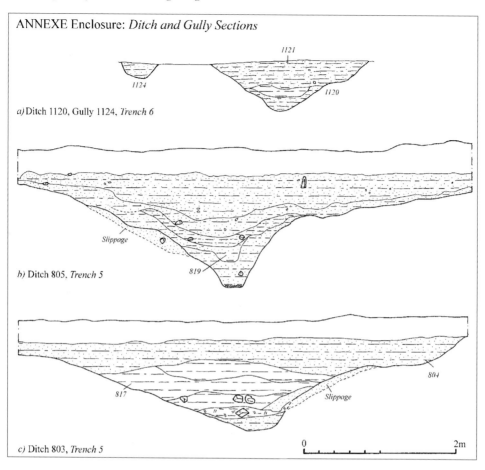

ANNEXE Enclosure: *Ditch and Gully Sections*

a) Ditch 1120, Gully 1124, *Trench 6*

b) Ditch 805, *Trench 5*

c) Ditch 803, *Trench 5*

33 Annexe enclosure: ditch and gully sections on the north side (trenches 5 & 6)

by a very substantial spoil heap, so that it became impractical to attempt to confirm this. The northern ditch also followed a somewhat sinuous course further to the west at the point where the annexe seems to have been subdivided (35) before continuing in a straight line due west and beyond the area available for examination. Despite this eccentric alignment, superficially suggestive of more than one phase in the laying out of the enclosure, the annexe appears to be a unitary conception, though with some amendments towards the end of its life (below).

In the absence of evidence to the contrary, it is also is assumed to be of one build with the fort. The change in alignment of the road just after it left the west gate of the fort was thought prior to excavation to indicate the possibility that the annexe was a later addition. However, examination of the road at that point gave no indication of it being other than a single construction. No clear explanation is apparent for this phenomenon, paralleled also at the east gate where the road turns sharply to the north immediately outside the ditches. It may have been intended as a further defensive measure, designed to prevent a head on charge along the road against one of the main gates. However, the

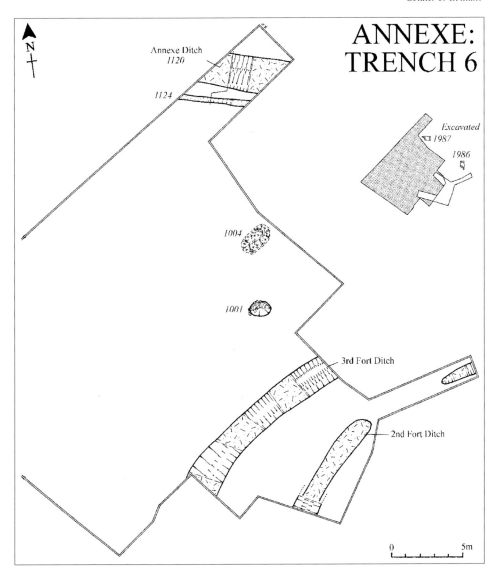

34 Plan of annexe trench 6 showing outer ditch continuing and internal revetment

change of alignment seems both too slight and too far removed from the fort gate to have been effective as such. Similar slight changes are attested at a number of later Antonine Wall forts, notably Mumrills, Balmuildy, Old Kilpatrick, Westerwood and Croy Hill, where they seem simply to reflect a minor adjustment in the alignment of the Military Way as it reaches the fort.

Although the change of alignment in the enclosing annexe ditches on the north side coincided with the point of later subdivision, this separation of an inner and outer area, the former some 2.4 acres (0.96ha) in extent, may have been part of the original layout since the later dividing ditch (chapter seven) is mirrored in places by an earlier shallow

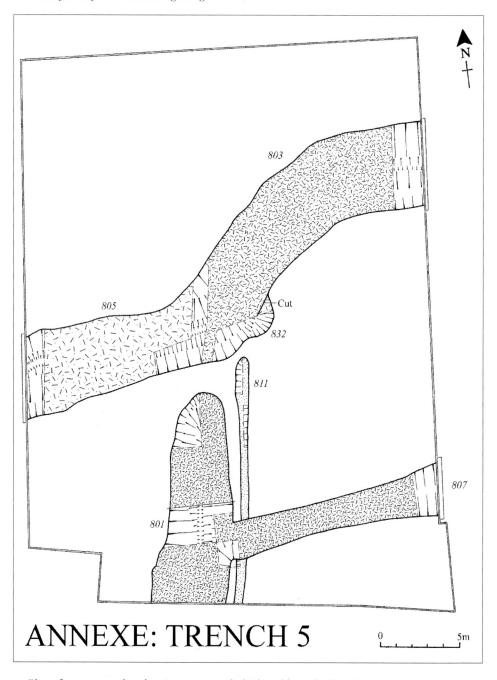

ANNEXE: TRENCH 5

35 Plan of annexe trench 5 showing outer north ditch and later dividing ditch

gully. Such lateral divisions are not commonly attested, though aerial photographs of the broadly contemporary forts at Easter Happrew and Dalswinton show similar features.

Activity within the annexe appears to focus on the road which emerges from the west gate of the fort (*36*). Utilisation of this area is concentrated, varied and subject to considerable change in a relatively short life span (see below). Away from the road there is much less intensive activity, though traces of at least one building were recovered. This contrast cannot be explained away as merely a reflection of the bias in the areas chosen for examination, since these were determined to a large extent on the basis of the results of the geophysical survey which itself indicated such a contrast.

FUNCTION OF THE ANNEXE

The traditional interpretation of the function of annexes is to see them as ancillary enclosures for pack animals, wagons in transit or for industrial activities. However, in an examination of the evidence for civil settlements (*vici*) outside forts, Sebastian Sommer argued that many annexes were, in effect, defended *vici*. Largely as a result of this assertion, we have seen the establishment of what has become almost a new orthodoxy, whereby defended *vici* are regarded as a relatively common occurrence and annexes are simply assumed to be civilian in character. Such a fundamental debate about the function of fort annexes thrives on a lack of information. Despite the number of examples known, there has been surprisingly little examination or, indeed, detailed consideration of them. In the standard introductory volume on Roman forts by Anne Johnson, for example, they receive no mention whatsoever. Accordingly, the detailed evidence from Elginhaugh assumes considerable importance in addressing this contentious issue.

It would seem that the ditches and assumed rampart surrounding the annexe at Elginhaugh were intended primarily simply to demarcate it, to contain rather than to exclude, favouring its interpretation as an ancillary enclosure. Compared to the number, size and profile of the ditches surrounding the fort, those which defined the annexe hardly warrant the term defences. Indeed, the number of ditches surrounding annexes at Flavian sites is not infrequently less than around the forts to which they are attached, as for example in the east annexe at Dalswinton, in the south annexe at Milton, at Hayton, Mollins (*colour plate 4*), Oakwood, Stracathro and Pen Llystyn. In the latter case, the excavated dimensions of the annexe ditch are also much smaller than those of the ditches surrounding the fort. Nor is any allowance made for the existence of the annexe in terms of the defences of the fort at Elginhaugh. The same number of ditches is present on the west side of the fort as elsewhere around its perimeter, further emphasising the distinction between fort and annexe. A similar relationship is apparent at Dalswinton, Newstead and Stracathro. The general pattern, however, is not entirely consistent. At two Flavian sites in Scotland, Malling and Cargill, the annexe is separated from the fort by only its rampart, suggesting that the two may have been more integrally linked, though these two sites are also exceptional in having multiple ditches defining the annexe itself. A similar close relationship may be indicated at other sites where the number of ditches

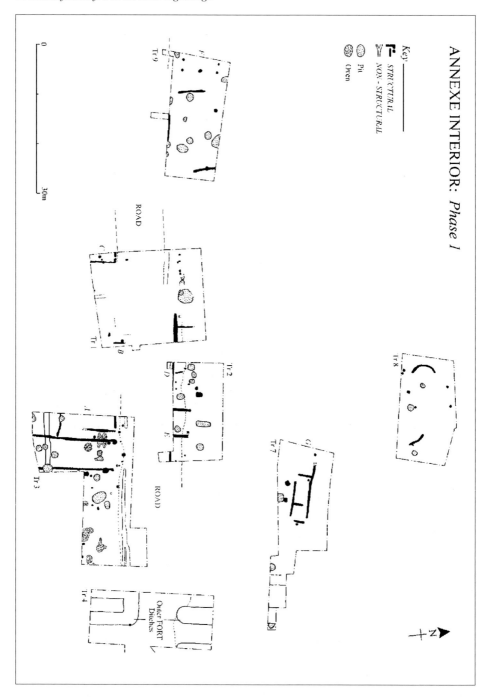

36 Elginhaugh: annexe interior, phase 1

surrounding the fort was reduced on the side facing the annexe, as at Strageath. So the relationship between fort and annexe at this period is not entirely consistent and this evidence alone is not sufficient to determine the function of annexes.

Turning to the evidence from the interior of the annexe at Elginhaugh, activity focuses on the road and undergoes considerable change in the relatively short period of time that the fort was occupied (above, chapter two). Trying to link together the various elements into phases of contemporary activity is rather like trying to do a jig-saw puzzle without the overall picture and with many of the pieces missing. Although a number of stratigraphic relationships are quite clear, much of this phasing rests on several assumptions. Where specific features have no stratigraphic associations, as is the case with many of the pits and individual post holes, they have been phased on the basis of analogy, juxtaposition or general probability. Inevitably, therefore, some will have been incorrectly attributed. In terms of chronology this has only limited repercussions given the very brief occupation span of the site. But even in relation to the interpretation of the function of the annexe, any such minor adjustment would not substantially affect the overall picture.

The occupation of the annexe is divided into two main phases, the first divided into three sub-phases which are considered here (the second main phase is discussed in chapter seven), but it should not be assumed that the changes which characterise each sub-phase were necessarily entirely synchronous. Given the variety of activities involved, it seems likely that some of the developments would have been more piecemeal, particularly in relation to the use of pits and oven or kiln structures. Nonetheless, phase 1 must be divided into at least two subdivisions since in trench 3 one building (A) and one oven (496) cannot be contemporary. Nor can two distinct forms of oven structure (e.g. 741 and 416) (*37*). A minimum of three sub-phases is preferred for a variety of reasons. Firstly, because one oven base (423) in trench 3 seems unlikely to have been housed within building A, but on spatial grounds appears to relate to other ovens to the east, two of which cannot be primary. Secondly, pit 459 in trench 3 cuts the east wall of building A, but is clearly not a demolition pit, while in turn the central construction slot of building A overlies the demarcation gully (425).

The primary road was 4m wide and extremely solidly constructed, made up of a primary dump of compacted sandy gravel and pebbles up to 0.21m thick with a concreted upper surface laid directly above the turf of the old ground surface (*38* and *colour plate 21*). It was extensively resurfaced during this first phase of occupation, with the addition of a further layer of compacted gravel which had the effect of widening the road as well as increasing the height of the camber.

The main primary features identified alongside the road, all located on its south side, were a series of ovens or kilns and associated pits. The best-preserved oven lay at the west end of trench 3 (*39*). It consisted of a central sub-rectangular firing pit with flues at each corner forming an H-shaped structure with its long axis east–west. The flues were partly defined by sandstone slabs and clay lined, the lining continuing a short distance into the firing pit, narrowing the connecting neck. The clay lining was fired orange-red from frequent use and the firing pit was full of ash, charcoal and small quantities of carbonised

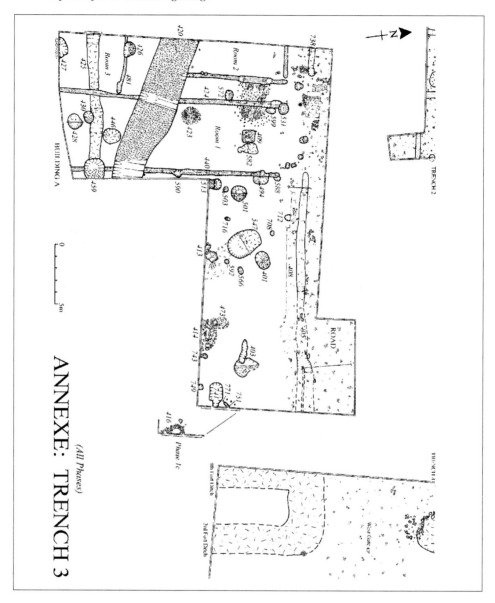

37 Plan of annexe trench 3

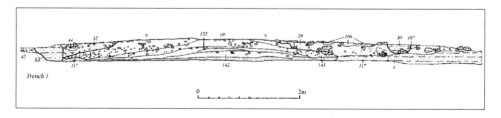

38 Section through the road, annexe trench 1

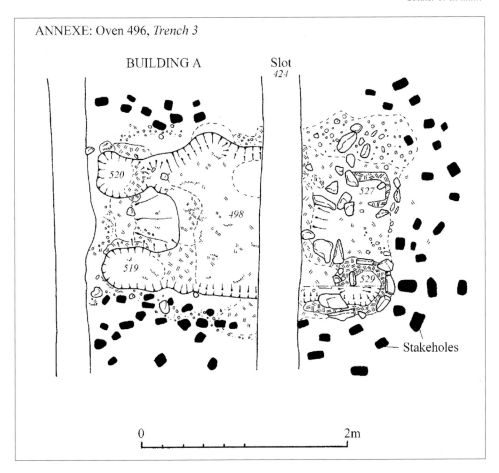

ANNEXE: Oven 496, *Trench 3*

BUILDING A

Slot
424

520

498

519

527

529

Stakeholes

0   2m

39 Annexe: detailed plan of oven (496), trench 3

seeds. The temperatures attained, however, were relatively low, for only the first 30–40mm of the clay lining had been fired and discoloration of the subsoil beyond from heat penetration was limited. Moreover, the superstructure, of unfired or partially fired clay, appeared to have been pushed down into the flues. Immediately surrounding the kiln was an irregular double row of stake holes averaging 0.1m in cross-section and 0.1m deep, presumably intended to support some form of raised platform or floor rather than merely a wind break. This, and the presence of charred emmer, spelt, barley and oats, along with larger quantities of unidentifiable cereal grains in the firing pit, would seem to indicate that the most likely function of this structure was a grain-drying oven.

Indeed, the H-shaped layout is not dissimilar to the surviving sub-floor remains built in stone of grain-drying ovens from villa sites of the third and fourth centuries AD in Lowland England. The function of such ovens has been debated in recent years and a reinterpretation of them as malting ovens for brewing beer put forward on the basis of experimental reconstruction work. However, the criteria for the differentiation of oven function in relation to the nature of the associated charred grain assemblage was established by Hillam

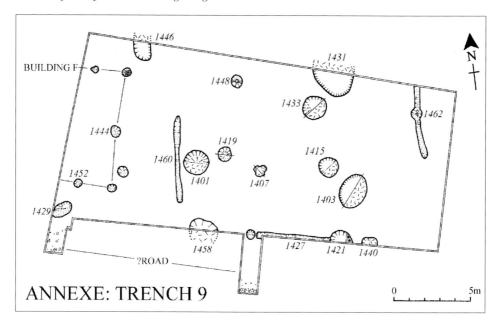

40 Plan of annexe trench 9

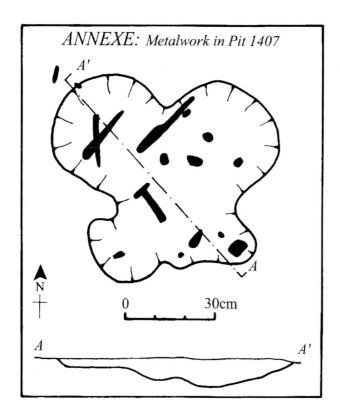

41 Detailed plan and profile of metalwork pit 1407, trench 9

and, though there are a number of sites where the associated grain assemblages indicated malt production, there are rather more examples which confirm the traditional function of these structures as grain driers. In damp climates in particular the need to dry grain before storage, to prevent germination and discourage the growth of moulds, is undeniable and well attested in medieval and early modern accounts from Ireland and northern Scotland.

A group of simpler oven or kiln-like structures was situated at the eastern end of trench 3 (see *37*), though only one was completely exposed as the rest lay in large part beyond the area under excavation. The most completely excavated example consisted of a large oval stokehole or firing pit with a narrow channel or flue extending out from its west side (403), both showing clear signs of burning *in situ* and filled with ash and charcoal (*colour plate 22*). A second similar example was situated nearby in the south-east corner of the trench (741). A possible third example was represented by the very shallow remains of the end of a further flue channel nearby (751). A group of at least four stake holes were noted curving round the north side of the structure, reminiscent of those surrounding the grain-drying oven. Finally, the ends of two further very similar flue channels (743 and 749) projected north from the southern edge of the trench. The precise function of this group of ovens is not immediately obvious. They are all similar in character, with a single flue channel and stokehole, and show signs of burning *in situ*, but only one had any trace of associated structural features. Though a sample from one flue did contain carbonised grain, including a few grains of barley, there were insufficient plant remains to lend much support to its interpretation as a grain-drying oven. The significance of the single burnt fish vertebra, not identifiable to species, from the flue of the most fully excavated example remains enigmatic, but would not alone seem sufficient to justify their identification as field ovens. The slight remains of the base of a more standard form of cooking oven (473), consisting of an oval patch of fired and unfired clay, were identified immediately to the west of the above group of five ovens. They lie partly beneath, but offset from, a later and better preserved example (414). Associated rake-out material contained ash, charcoal and carbonised cereal remains, though not in any great quantity. This area of ovens or kilns seems to have been cordoned off from the rest of the annexe to the south of the road by a shallow flat-bottomed gully running parallel to the road at a distance of some 18m. Its clean silty sand infill with pebbles perhaps suggests that it served also as a drain or soakaway.

Several pits, mainly of uncertain function, were dotted around the area both to the north and south of the road in trenches 2 and 3. They were not particularly rich in finds, though one deep sub-rectangular pit example (248) may have been a rubbish pit for it contained quantities of coarse pottery and burnt animal bone (sheep/goat and cattle). Pits also characterised the most westerly area examined alongside the road on its north side in trench 9 (*40*). There were also possible traces of iron working. An irregular, shallow, quadri-lobate depression (1407) contained quantities of iron objects, mainly nails or unidentifiable fragments, but including a T-bar and two crossed rods, and small spherical metallic droplets recovered from the environmental sampling of its silty sand fill, which may represent a dump of waste from metal working, though the feature showed no sign of burning *in situ* (*41*). An adjacent rubbish pit (1433) contained coal and some iron slag, as well as a mason's wedge, and may be associated.

42 Obverse and reverse of a slightly worn *as* of Domitian AD 85 from the annexe road makeup.
Copyright: Hunterian Museum and Art Gallery, University of Glasgow

Thus, this primary phase of use of the annexe (1a) consisted of what might be termed industrial production or materials processing, involving grain drying, iron working and rubbish deposition. Evidence of industrial activity, that is processes characterised by pits, ovens and furnaces, is not infrequently attested in the limited investigation of annexe interiors that has taken place. In the southern annexe of the Antonine fort at Camelon, a number of hearths or furnaces for iron working were located in an area riddled with pits. The numerous pits and wells uncovered in the early excavations within the annexes at Newstead are rightly famous and excavations there in the late 1980s to early 90s indicated industrial activity taking place in part of the south annexe, involving hearths or furnaces, though interpreted by the excavators as civilian in character. A similar picture is also presented by remains uncovered in early excavations outside the fort at Templeborough in Yorkshire, and numerous pottery kilns and associated pits have been identified outside the vexillation fortress at Longthorpe, though apparently not within an enclosed annexe. There are, however, no ready parallels for grain processing being undertaken. On the basis of the coin evidence (below), this phase of industrial activity lasted for most of the life of the fort, continuing until at least AD 85.

The start of the next phase (1b) was heralded by a further resurfacing of the road, which seems to have had the effect of shifting it slightly to the north while reducing its overall width by 0.4m. The new road surface, up to 0.25m thick made up of slightly larger stones, but somewhat less well compacted, sealed the first resurfacing but survived only towards the sides of the road (see *38* and *colour plate 21*). Within the make-up layer was a very slightly worn *as* of Domitian, probably dating to AD 85, providing a *terminus post quem* for this phase (*42*). The new road surface was accompanied by a more general spread of gravel to both the north and south, though this survived for no more than 4.0m from the road on either side. This surface seems best interpreted as providing a base level for the series of timber strip buildings, associated with storage pits, which characterise this phase of activity, even though some of their construction trenches cut through it. No complete buildings were uncovered within the limits of the area examined, but there were at least six (A-F), and possibly eight,

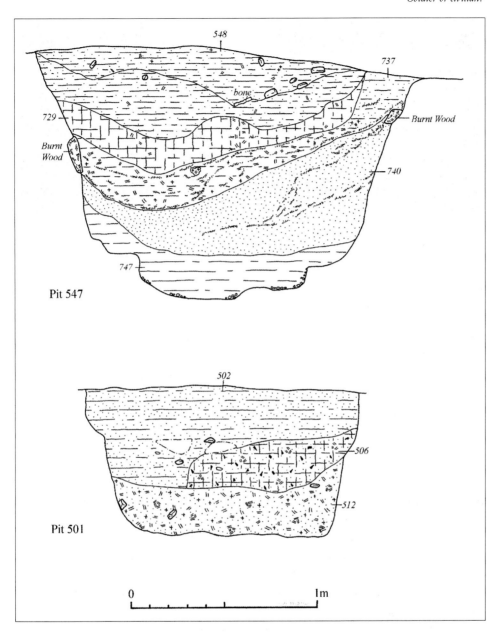

43 Sections through pits 547 & 501, annexe trench 3

depending on how the elements were linked together. These buildings were located on both sides of the road (see *36*) and aligned approximately north to south fronting directly onto it.

The most extensively uncovered building (A) on the south side of the road in trench 3 was fronted by a verandah or fence. It consisted of a single large open-fronted room (1) to the east, separated from a closed room (2) to the west by a passageway, which also led to a third room at the rear (see *37*). The only internal feature was a rectangular pit (409), lined with sandstone slabs some of which had collapsed into its interior, almost centrally positioned in room 1. Its original function is unclear, but its fill contained quantities of carbonised grain, some of which had sprouted, fragments of lava quernstone and what may have been copper alloy metalworking debris. The filling spilled out across the floor of the building, suggesting that it represents material dumped during demolition.

At least two of the nearby pits to the east of building A appear to have been in contemporary use. Pit 547 was large, some 1.3m deep, with near vertical sides and an almost flat bottom (43). Fragments of burnt wood recorded at two points on the side may derive from a lining. A group of four small post holes appear to cluster around the pit and may have formed a support for some form of tripod lifting device, reminiscent of the arrangement surrounding the well in the *principia* (above, chapter three). Some form of storage function, perhaps even for water, seems likely, for the pit certainly penetrated the modern water table. The lower fills consisted of clean, wet, silty sand, above which were demolition-derived fills containing large quantities of charcoal, carbonised cereal remains and fragments of burnt wattle and daub, presumably from the demolition of building A. A second pit (501) was sub-rectangular with nearly vertical sides and a flat bottom (43). Quantities of purple clay in the lower fills suggested that it may originally have been lined, though no trace of a clay lining was found *in situ*. The other notable feature of the upper fills was the presence of quantities of good quality coal. Again some storage function seems likely, perhaps even for coal.

Traces of other buildings fronting onto the road were very slight. All that was uncovered of building B was part of one wall and only the north-east corner of building C was located, both in trench 1 (44). Similarly only fragmentary remains survived of buildings D and E, fronting onto the road on its north side in trench 2, making it difficult to determine precisely how many structures were involved (44). Once again, however, a number of pits are likely to have been associated with the buildings. Pit 236, located between buildings D and E, was sub-rectangular in plan with near vertical sides and a flat bottom. The form of the pit and its primary fill of clean silty sand suggest some storage function, though the presence of abundant pottery and other artefacts, including bovine teeth, unidentified cereal grains and quantities of charcoal in the upper fills may derive from its subsequent re-use as a rubbish pit. Similarly located, and aligned with its long axis at right angles to the road, a narrow rectangular pit (240) had clearly been lined, perhaps with wattle and daub. A layer of dark silty sand with concentrations of finely comminuted charcoal and burnt daub fragments, containing quantities of pottery and other finds, covered the bottom of the pit and continued up its sides. Above this was a layer of clean sand and above that a layer of demolition infill, again rich in finds. The function of this pit is uncertain, though storage is a strong possibility. Traces of buildings were also recovered on the north side the road further west in trench 9 (see 40). The clearest example (building F) at the western end of the trench was defined by five post holes outlining a rectangle. The other building remains in the trench consisted of disconnected slots and occasional post holes, none of which combined to make any coherent structure.

1 Aerial photograph of the site of Elginhaugh taken at the time of its discovery in 1979, showing the line of the Roman road with its T-junction

2 View across the fort from the west after first stage machine stripping and manual cleaning, with only the *via principalis* and adjacent drain visible

3 Barrack 2 during secondary stripping from the west, the officers' end

Above: 4 Ditches outlining the small fort or large fortlet at Mollins from the air, revealed as positive cropmarks

Below: 5 Part of the coin hoard after cleaning. *Copyright: Hunterian Museum and Art Gallery*

Above: 6 Pit 2425 in barrack 12 showing upper demolition fill

Below: 7 Nail pit under excavation, barrack 9

8 Extant oak post in the north gate

9 East gate and water-filled ditches beyond during excavation, from the west

10 West–south–west interval tower showing clay rampart material sealing post pits

11 Granary (*horreum*) 1 from the east

Left: 12 Barrack 10 completely excavated, from the south

Below: 13 Woven-wattle lining of the well in the headquarters building (*principia*)

Opposite: 14 The workshop (*fabrica*) from the north

15 Reconstructed timber gateway, the Lunt, Baginton, Coventry

16 South gate at Carlisle during excavation, showing surviving threshold beam and timber-lined drain

Right: 17 South-west corner tower

Below: 18 General view of the headquarters building (*principia*) under excavation, from the south

19 Latrine pit and stone base in room 5 of the commanding officer's house (*praetorium*)

20 Reconstructed timber granary, the Lunt, Baginton, Coventry

21 Section through the road, annexe trench 1

22 East end of the annexe, trench 3, showing ovens 416, 414, 413 (phase 1c) and 403 (phase 1a) on the south side of the road

23 Bank of ovens and associated features in the south-west corner

Above: 24 Post-fort oven (2432) overlying the intervallum road to the south of the west gate.

Below: 25 Clay packed slighting ditch, west gate

26 Annexe gateway post holes cutting through road surface, trench 1

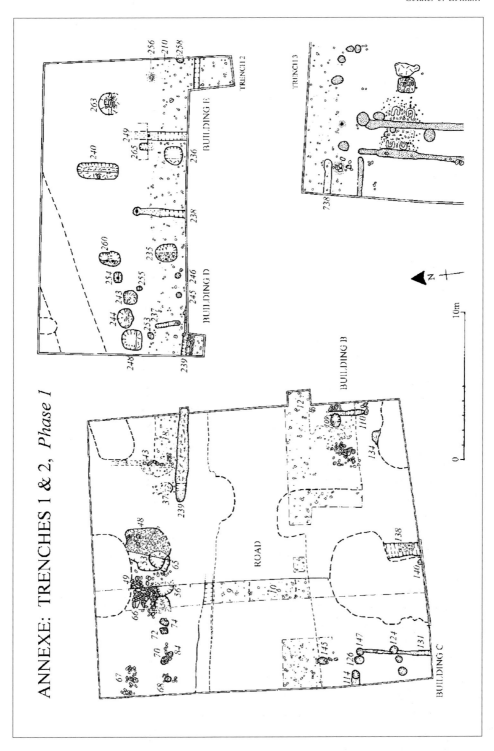

44 Plan of annexe trenches 1 & 2, phase 1: buildings and pits

Finally, the only substantive feature exposed in the interior of the annexe away from the road line was a rectangular building (G) in trench 7, aligned east–west parallel to the road (see *36*). This, too, was probably associated with a series of pits, though no stratigraphical relationship could be established.

All the buildings on both sides of the road are assumed to be contemporary, for in no case do they overlap spatially or, apart from minor repairs, show signs of more than one phase of construction. They clearly, however, mark a major change of function within this area of the annexe. Despite the difficulty of identifying separate buildings from the fragments uncovered, in general they appear to be of the simple rectangular 'strip' type which are commonly found in civilian settlements outside forts and in the so-called 'small towns', though usually of stone construction. Contemporary analogies in timber are provided by the first phase buildings in the civil settlement outside the Flavian fort at Carlisle. However, this should not be taken to indicate that the buildings were of specifically civilian form and lead to suggestions that at this stage in its life the annexe became a defended *vicus*, for similar buildings are also known within military establishments, such as the contemporary base at Corbridge, Red House, and the earlier fort at Oberstimm in Raetia. Open-fronted store buildings (*tabernae*) of similar form line the *via principalis* and *via praetoria* in the contemporary legionary fortress at Inchtuthil and, indeed, such buildings are commonly attested in legionary fortresses, though not always identified as store buildings. That it is more difficult to find close analogies for these buildings from within annexes is primarily a reflection of the lack of investigation of these attached enclosures. However, relatively simple rectangular timber buildings are attested in the first phase of the annexe outside the fort at Carlisle and similar buildings are also known from excavation in the various annexes at Newstead, though interpreted by the excavators as civilian, while more fragmentary remains were noted in the north annexe at Camelon.

A storage or workshop function seems to be the most appropriate identification for the examples excavated at Elginhaugh. The location of a stone-lined pit, associated with both metalworking debris and burnt grain, in the centre of room 1 in building A lends some support to both interpretations, though the frequency with which cereal remains were recovered from demolition deposits generally is quite striking. The presence of associated storage pits, perhaps for coal and water, outside the buildings is, however, more indicative of some form of industrial activity.

There was clear evidence that the buildings had been demolished and their remains burnt. A spread of demolition material, consisting of burnt daub and charcoal overlay the phase 1b road surface in trench 1, while a thin layer of charcoal was noted in the upper fill of the front wall slot of building D. Demolition material in the form of charcoal and burnt daub was recovered from the roadside drain (405); the primary demarcation gully in trench 1; and from the upper fills of several pits. Furthermore, two pits in trench 3 (401, 426) may have been dug as part of the demolition process, since both are filled primarily with demolition material and pit 426 cuts one of the construction trenches of building A (see *37*).

The third phase of occupation in the annexe which followed their demolition was again marked by the resurfacing of the road and a return to activities involving fire.

Slightly coarser and less compacted than earlier surfaces, a layer of sandy gravel was recorded towards the sides of the road abutting a kerb of larger stones in trench 1. Ovens or kilns were located on both sides of the road, though best attested by the group of four in a line (413, 414, 416 and 423) to the south of it in trench 3 (see *37* and *colour plate 22*), spaced at regular intervals not quite parallel with the road. Assuming a fifth example in an area not examined, the spacing between the ovens was almost exactly 6m, centre to centre. The most completely exposed example (423) consisted of a sub-circular base made up of rounded cobbles embedded in clay reddened by oxidisation. The other three were only partly visible, as they extended beyond the edges of the trench, but were broadly similar in character. They are similar in form and construction to the standard cooking ovens regularly found within forts (below, chapter seven), though slightly smaller. The remains of a further fragmentary oven (48) were noted to the north of the road in trench 1 (*44*) with an area of light cobbling and sandstone slabs (49), which may have served as an associated working surface, immediately to the west. A group of sub-circular pits (446, 430, 428, 459 and 427) at the southern extremity of trench 3 may also relate to this phase (see *37*), along with a group of pits and shallow depressions in trench 9 (see *40*), for they break up the alignment of the structural remains along the edge of the road.

It is not clear why it was deemed necessary to extend cooking activities into the annexe, unless it was a reflection of the pressure for space within the fort, though with a slight reduction in the garrison towards the end of the occupation (chapter four) the timing seems somewhat belated. Alternatively, the ovens may have served some unspecified industrial purpose, though this does not appear to have involved the working of metals and they do not seem to possess the characteristic features of pottery kilns. Perhaps they simply relate to temporary occupation during the demolition of the fort.

While the different elements represented in all three sub-phases of the use of the annexe might well be found in a civilian context, the dramatic and fairly rapidly changing character of the activity smacks more of a response to short-term military needs than to the establishment and development of a civil settlement. Indeed, the first main phase (1a), with its absence of buildings and emphasis on materials processing, is precisely what might be expected in an ancillary military enclosure. Even the type of buildings involved in phase 1b, arguably characteristic of civil settlements, is well paralleled inside forts. Away from the main road, both excavation and geophysical survey indicated that the intensity of occupation was much reduced. Even the ubiquitous pits were limited in number. Only one building was detected, of rather different character to those alongside the road, perhaps functioning as an office or store. Though other minor structural remains were identified, they did not define buildings, but are best interpreted as forming a rail fence to provide a picket line for horses. Thus, much of the annexe appears to have been neither encumbered with buildings nor used for any form of industrial activity. It may have served as a wagon park or possibly an area in which to tether or graze horses, as others have postulated. Similar activities are attested in the Flavian phases of the south annexe at Newstead, which is characterised as largely given over to open spaces for stockpiling bulky commodities or corralling animals. A primary function as a wagon park for goods in transit seems the best interpretation of the main annexe at Oxton, given its huge size in relation to the fortlet to which it is attached. Its location at the midpoint on the road from Newstead to Elginhaugh just before Dere Street begins the climb over Turf Law, Dun Law and Soutra Hill, lends further support to such an interpretation, though on current evidence the site seems more likely to be Antonine than Flavian in date.

In summary, the evidence from Elginhaugh would seem to conform to the more traditional interpretation of the function of annexes as ancillary military enclosures for a variety of essential functions not readily undertaken within the fort itself, such as the housing of animals or goods in transit, food processing or minor industrial activities. It is clear that the activity taking place alongside the road was intensive, not merely as reflected in the density of the remains and the fairly rapid changes attested, but because of the number of times it was felt necessary to resurface the road itself. A similar picture has been obtained from limited excavation in the annexe of the fort at Carlisle, where during the Flavian occupation over a somewhat longer period of around twenty or twenty-five years (periods 2-4a) intensive usage involving a variety of activities is attested, including storage and the housing of animals, with quite frequent changes of site layout, alternating between buildings and open areas. A similar conclusion, that they served multifunctional military purposes, housing various types of semi-industrial activities and some official buildings, was reached by Geoff Bailey in his detailed analysis of the evidence for annexes attached to forts on the Antonine Wall during the second-century re-occupation of the area.

Indeed, despite the current orthodoxy that annexes were enclosed civil settlements, there are several wider reasons why all annexes should be regarded as primarily for military rather than civilian use, unless there is strong evidence to the contrary. There is a growing number of examples of forts where attached annexes and adjacent civil settlements are both attested, as for example in north-west Wales at Tomen-y-Mur, Caer Gai, Cefn Caer and Caerhun, and in northern England at Carlisle and Castleford. This implies that the two were intended to serve different purposes. Furthermore, several sites have multiple annexes, notably Dalswinton, Milton, Newstead and Oxton, which seem more likely to reflect varied and changing military use than civilian settlement. Indeed, some temporary camps in Scotland have annexes, indicating that the separation of certain military activities from the main accommodation area for the troops was sometimes considered to be a necessity even during campaigning.

This is not to suggest that there was not a civilian presence associated with the fort at Elginhaugh. The only hint of it, however, is provided by the analysis of the mortaria, which indicates local manufacture of products for military use, since such manufacture is generally regarded as associated with specialist civilian potters rather than being undertaken directly by the military (below, chapter six).

SIX

LIFE ON THE EDGE OF EMPIRE

What does the archaeological evidence from Elginhaugh tell us about daily life for the garrison living in what was at the time of its foundation one of Rome's most northerly military outposts?

WARFARE

The garrison was first and foremost a military force, tasked with contributing to the continuing conquest, defending the province, controlling the local area and maintaining the peace. These activities are not, however, immediately recognisable in the archaeological evidence from its base. We would not expect large quantities of armour or weaponry to be recovered, for example, since these were prized possessions not readily disposed of and subject to repair or recycling. Nonetheless, a limited amount of weaponry and other military equipment was recovered which hints at this martial activity and shows something of its range and variety. The various pieces of copper alloy harness fittings for the horses have been referred to already (above, chapter four) (see *32*), but a number of fragments of copper alloy armour were also recovered, including the earguard from a helmet (no. 23), two incomplete pendants from aprons worn to protect the groin and lower abdomen (nos 26 and 27) and a fragment of *lorica segmentata*, the segmental plate armour normally associated with legionary troops, along with a number of iron buckles (e.g. nos 164 and 166) (*45*). A rounded leaf-shaped pendant (1) made from thin silver sheeting found in a demolition pit at the front of the *praetorium* may also have been armour or harness decoration, though it seems too fragile. Weaponry included a sword hilt guard and two dagger or knife guards, all of copper alloy, a range of iron weapons, including a shield boss, a wide selection of spearhead or arrowhead types (e.g. nos 117 and 119) and a number of ferrules (e.g. no. 124), the pointed butt ends of spear shafts (*46*). A surviving ink writing tablet from the broadly contemporary Flavian fort at Carlisle is a report from a decurion of the *ala Gallorum Sebosiana*, possibly the unit which had earlier been in garrison at Elginhaugh, to his commanding officer listing missing weaponry. It implies that each cavalry trooper would have been armed with a lance, two smaller javelins and a sword.

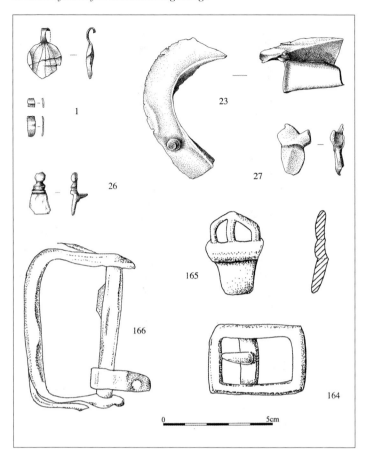

45 Various copper alloy
and iron armour pieces

Most unexpected, however, was the discovery of two copper alloy catapult fittings: a washer and part of a linear ratchet mechanism (47). Catapults were built according to strict rules of calibration. These determined the dimensions of the washers, which were set into counter plates with levers used to twist and tighten the torsion springs. The Elginhaugh example, with an inner diameter of 35mm, is one of the two smallest recorded archaeologically across the whole of the Roman Empire and must have come from a hand-held weapon similar in use and effect to a medieval crossbow, but based on the principle of torsion rather than tension providing the firepower. The existence of such hand-held weapons in the Roman army was only seriously mooted in 1999, and is now further supported by the discovery of a near complete metal frame from one such weapon at the legionary fortress of Xanten in Germany. However, ongoing study by Tracey Rihll, reassessing the literary sources and identifying the associated shot in museum collections currently wrongly identified as slingshot, suggests that they may have been much more common than has previously been supposed. The linear ratchet mechanism is a rectangular bar with a T-sectioned channel down one face with a series of transverse angled ribs used to hold the mechanism in place after it was cocked. This is the first linear ratchet, as opposed to a circular ratchet, found so far in the Roman world.

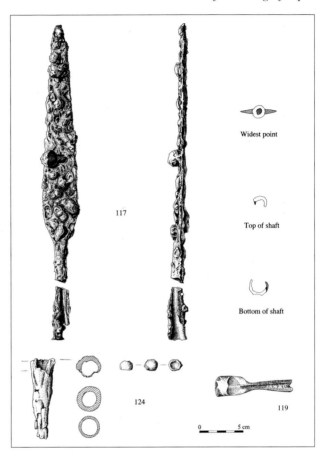

Widest point

Top of shaft

Bottom of shaft

117

124

119

0   5 cm

46 Iron spearheads and ferrules

It may have come from the same catapult as the washer, but it is perhaps improbable that only two elements would have survived of something as substantial as a catapult if the weapon had been abandoned complete; it is more likely that the pieces had been stripped from their wooden mountings for recycling as raw metal or replacement parts. However, if the ratchet did come from the same piece as the washer, then that weapon must have been a hand-held torsion weapon. Alternatively, it may have come from a powerful form of composite bow, a tension weapon, which would have been cocked by thrusting the stomach against the crescent-shaped concavity at the rear of the stock, though arming it by the thrust of the leg might be more appropriate for cavalry. These two distinctive pieces of metalwork are the first archaeological confirmation of such sophisticated weaponry being utilised by a cavalry unit, though Arrian refers to cavalry firing darts from a 'machine' in his second-century AD treatise on military tactics. The presence of such small artillery pieces reminds us also of the need for training, particularly in the use of specialised weaponry.

The context of the recovery of this armour and weaponry gives little clue as to the nature of its loss. Most of the pieces derived from disturbed or demolition contexts, such as the helmet ear guard, spearhead and catapult washer from the upper demolition

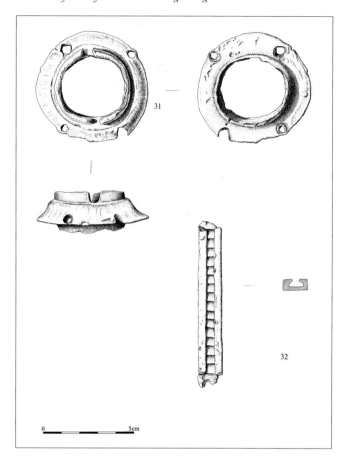

47 Catapult washer and linear ratchet mechanism

fill of the well in *principia*, presumably discarded as damaged or surplus to requirements on abandonment of the fort. However, accidental loss should not be entirely discounted and might explain the fragment of *lorica segmentata* found in the grain-drying oven in the annexe (above, chapter four).

Disposal of worn out or damaged uniforms or equipment is the most likely explanation for the recovery of shoes and even pieces of tent leather (*48*) from waterlogged contexts at the bottom of the ditches outside the east gate. The shoe fragments from the ditch deposits all belong to the so-called *caliga* type of military cowhide or calfskin boot, which is typical of first-century military provision and has a D-shaped nailing pattern on the sole (no. 2) and an open lattice-like upper (*49*). The surviving fragments of uppers were very tiny, but one complete left sole, size 5.5, was recovered.

Several copper alloy brooches (*fibulae*) were also found (*50*). These were mainly bow and trumpet brooches, which are common finds on military sites of the first and second centuries AD, along with one or two more unusual examples, including a plate brooch (no. 10) with a silver sheet attached to the face of a type rare in Britain, but occasionally found on the continent. Such brooches were used primarily to fasten together tunics or military cloaks and were not infrequently broken.

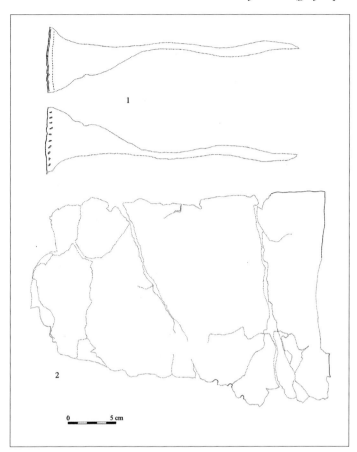

48 Leather tent pieces

CARE AND MAINTENANCE

One of the most time-consuming activities for the garrison would have been the general care and maintenance of the numerous cavalry mounts housed within the fort. The fact that they shared their accommodation emphasises the close link between man and horse. One of the noticeable features of the carbonised plant record from the site is the large amount of charred barley grains present within the fort. Various references in the classical authors indicate that barley was usually fed to horses and a surviving ink writing tablet from the contemporary Flavian fort at Carlisle records the actual allocation of three days supply of wheat and barley to the individual *turmae* in the cavalry garrison there. The identification of the remains of urine pits within the stable barracks (above, chapter four) and the occasional presence within the surviving macroplant evidence of possible animal bedding serve to remind us that mucking out would also have needed to be done on a daily basis.

The repair and maintenance of military equipment would also have been a regular task. At the most mundane level, several whetstones attest the need to keep knives and other blades sharp, while the repair of clothing is indicated by one iron sewing needle (*51*).

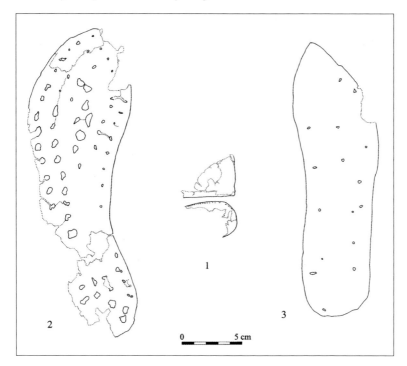

49 Leather shoes: 1) child's; 2) military *caliga*; 3) ladies *calceus*

Such iron needles rarely survive, but must have been quite common during the Roman period. Bone examples are more frequently recovered, though not from the more acidic soils which are common in Scotland.

The primary role of the workshop would have been repair of equipment on a larger scale. Positive evidence of metalworking within the building in the form of hammer scale was absent, though the regular use of fire was indicated and associated deposits were sufficiently iron rich to postulate smithing. The location of the building at the rear of the rampart in the north-east corner of the fort and its part stone walls would have reduced the risk of any fire spreading to the timber buildings in the interior (*colour plate 14*). Since the garrison of the fort has been identified as predominantly cavalry, provision of a smithy might reasonably be expected, but for the fact that Roman horses seem to have gone largely unshod. Nailed iron horseshoes were not in common use until the early medieval period, while the most commonly attested Roman horseshoe, the hipposandal, was a form of temporary shoe primarily for draught animals to give better grip on smooth metalled roads which was easily removed when not required. On the other hand, the need to repair ironwork, whether weaponry, tools or other equipment, is likely to have been a regular requirement in any military establishment.

Further traces of metalworking were recovered on the opposite side of the fort, to the north of the west gate. Here in the gap between the rampart and the intervallum road was an area of industrial activity which extended for some 15m from the back of the gate (*52*). This zone was created partly by a narrowing of the road and partly by the sharp inturn of the rampart to accommodate the recessed gateway. The metalworking

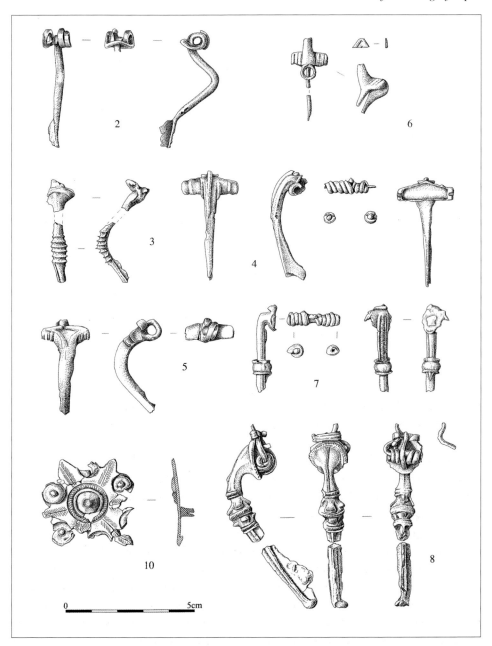

50 Various brooches (*fibulae*), mainly copper alloy

area lay in the lee of the rampart at the southern end of the zone and consisted of a spread of charcoal, clay, burnt stone, heavily corroded pieces of iron and numerous pieces of crucible or mould. An oval area of red clay sandwiched between thin layers of charcoal across the northern part of this spread may indicate the location of an open hearth. On its south-eastern edge, a shallow oval or horse-shoe shaped depression

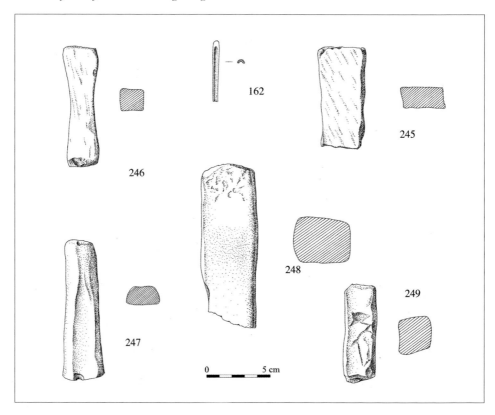

51 Whetstones and iron needle

edged with purple clay contained further crucible fragments. The undisturbed sand surrounding it was discoloured by the effects of heating, confirming its identification as a hearth or bowl furnace. These structural remains and numerous crucible fragments, some containing traces of copper alloy, combined with the presence of scattered bits of copper alloy in the immediate area in the form of both artefacts and waste, indicates that the small-scale manufacture or probably repair of copper alloy artefacts was taking place. Apparently associated with this activity immediately to the north was a simple open-ended timber building approximately 3m sq, set against the back of the rampart, which was subsequently replaced by a lean-to structure at least 5m long built on dry-stone foundations. A number of sandstone slabs towards the northern end of the building may indicate the provision of a stone floor.

Finally, a small but concentrated deposit of copper alloy metalworking residues was found towards the western corner of the southern range of the ambulatory in the headquarters building (*53*). Within a spread of fired clay, intermixed with charcoal, nails and other iron fragments, was a small cylinder-shaped crucible containing copper-based residues. The surprising location of this industrial activity may relate to its proximity to weapon stores (*armamentaria*) alongside the courtyard at the front of the headquarters building, as is attested at a number of other forts.

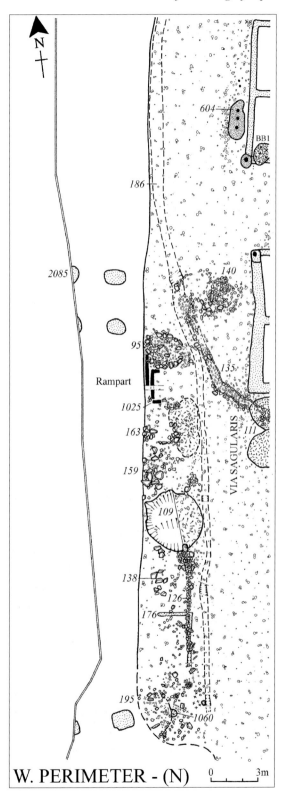

N

604
BB1

186

2085

140

95

Rampart

135

1025

163

111

159

109

138

126

176

195

1060

VIA SAGULARIS

52 Metalworking area at the rear of the west gate

W. PERIMETER - (N)

0   3m

53 Hearth with crucible for copper alloy working in the headquarters building (*principia*)

Given the existence of a structure identified as a workshop, it seems strange to find metalworking also taking place just behind the west gate only a few metres from the commanding officer's house and even more surprising that it should also have been taking place, even if only on a small scale, in the ambulatory at the front of the headquarters building. It is becoming increasingly apparent, however, that such small-scale industrial working is not infrequently found in various locations around a fort, usually in the *intervallum* area, though not necessarily inside any structure. Evidence of ironworking was identified in a similar location beside the north-east gate at Pen Llystyn and in the western *retentura* in the legionary fortress at Inchtuthil, while slag from pits elsewhere in the fortress, particularly along the *via decumana,* suggests that metalworking outside the workshop was not just confined to this one location. There are few parallels for the types of hearth represented since the limited examples excavated often provide little structural detail and those that do seem to show great variety. However, the oval clay hearth base by the west gate is reminiscent of an example from within the workshop at Red House, Corbridge which was associated with the working of copper alloy.

Ironworking was apparently also one of the activities which characterised the primary and most long-lived phase of use of the annexe (1a) (above, chapter five), particularly in trench 9 where one pit (see *41*) produced some iron slag. Evidence of industrial activity,

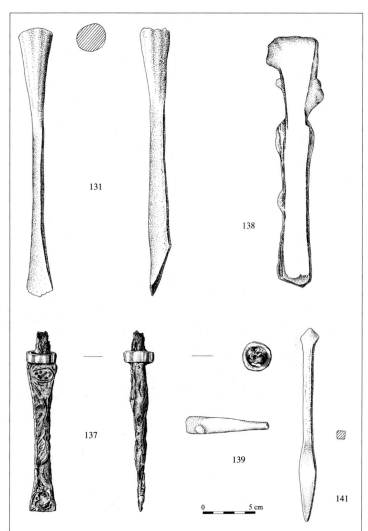

54 Iron builder's tools: crowbar (131); possible drill bit (141); mason's wedge (147); and three chisels (137-9)

that is processes characterised by pits, ovens and furnaces, is not infrequently attested in the limited investigation of other annexe interiors that has taken place, as for example at Camelon and Newstead.

While metalworking would have been a specialist activity, the repair of buildings probably involved larger numbers of troops. It too would have been undertaken on a regular basis (see above, chapter three, for examples of building repairs), particularly where the timber structures seem to have suffered from problems of rising damp, as was manifestly clear in the case of barrack 3 whose north wall at the officers' end seems to have been replaced several times. Such activity is further supported by the recovery of a number of builders' tools, including a crowbar (no. 131), a possible drill bit (no. 141), a mason's wedge (no. 147), the shoe of a small spade and at least three chisels (nos 137-9) (*54*), mainly from demolition contexts.

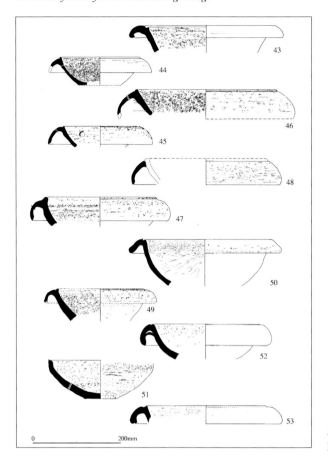

55 Mortaria types, including probable wasters 44-9

MANUFACTURE

Whether soldiers were directly involved in the local manufacture of any of their equipment is debated. There is absolutely no doubt, for example, that quite a high percentage of the coarseware pottery and mortaria (heavy mixing bowls) utilised in the fort was produced locally. Though no kilns have been discovered, there are a numbers of examples of mortaria which were seconds or wasters (55); that is, they had been imperfectly produced or misfired. Moreover, the rim profiles of these local products cannot be paralleled elsewhere in the same fabric, which is a cream or white ware rarely attested at military sites in Scotland. Indeed, there is no other evidence of such clay being exploited in Scotland in the Flavian period. Similar arguments apply also to the coarseware. Again there are numbers of wasters, vessels which appear to have suffered extensive damage, either from overfiring, or from a combination of poor manufacture and overfiring (56, nos 108-111). They have been so extensively damaged that they would not have been fit for exchange in any kind of market system and, therefore, should not have travelled far from the kiln site. These vessel types include small jars, a large bowl and a lid in one of four distinctive light-coloured fabrics.

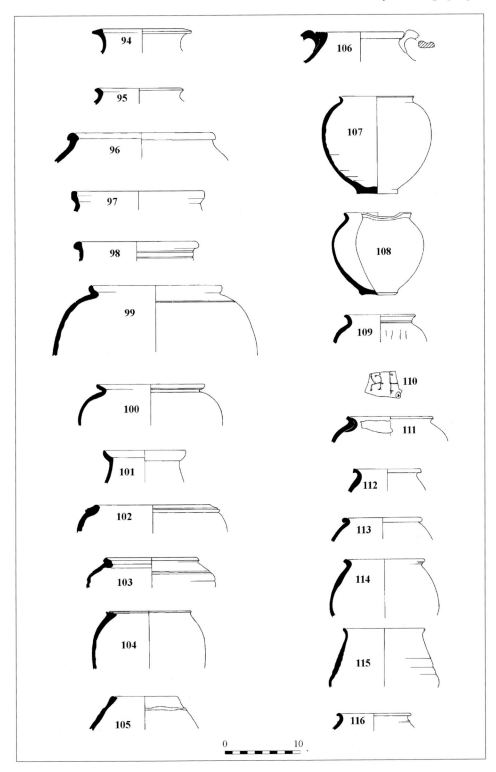

56 Coarseware jar types, including wasters (nos 108-111)

The sub-standard workmanship evident in the locally made coarseware suggests that it was never intended to compete in the commercial market, but was produced simply to compensate for deficiencies in long-distance supply, which also implies production by the military themselves for their own use. If this was the case, it would again have been a specialist activity, with only two or possibly three different potters apparently involved.

By contrast, the locally made mortaria indicate the activity of several different civilian potters of continental or southern British origin, some of whom can be precisely identified from the names stamped onto the rims of their products (57). Several local mortaria clearly show links in details of their form to the Verulamium region and particularly to the work of Albinus (nos 2-3), whose products are also represented at Elginhaugh. One of the potters involved is Borinianus (no. 13), a newly identified potter (though two examples of his mortaria made at Elginhaugh have now been recognised at Carlisle). Given the outstanding importance of Albinus in the mortarium industry in the Verulamium region in the Flavian period, it seems more than likely that he was personally involved in sending potters, including Borinianus, from one of his workshops to Elginhaugh. Although there are no stamps at Elginhaugh of S Valerius Viroma(rus?), who produced mortaria at Colchester, there is a very unusual form amongst the local material which is matched only by his products, suggesting that he too might have been involved in sending potters or even have gone to Elginhaugh himself. Finally, there is no doubt that two of the potters, Fronto and Boriedo (nos 14 and 15), hailed from the north of France on the basis of the parallels for their style of work, but in terms of production known to date, Boriedo is represented only by his mortaria from Elginhaugh. The collection of mortarium producers attested working at Elginhaugh, coming from at least three different centres of production in southern England and the continent, serves to emphasise the commercial importance of the military market for this specialised form of wide bowl used for the preparation of food, distinguished by its heavy rim, pouring spout and grits lining the internal surface. Since no pottery kilns were identified in the annexe, either in the area excavated or suggested by the wider geophysical investigation, these were presumably located outside, as might be expected for production activity not under direct military control.

Finally, there is some suggestion that broken glass was being collected for recycling at Elginhaugh, though whether this was done by the soldiers during the occupation of the fort or by the indigenous population after the abandonment is unclear. None of the vessels recovered could be reconstructed from the surviving fragments, and most were represented by only a single fragment, although some of these are quite large.

ADMINISTRATION

The Roman army was no less of a bureaucratic organisation than any other army. One of the official activities for which evidence is generally only rarely recovered is record keeping. Despite the occasional waterlogged conditions prevailing, there are no writing tablets recorded from the site, such as those recovered from the forts at Carlisle and Vindolanda. However, the recovery of one iron stylus and four samian inkwells mainly

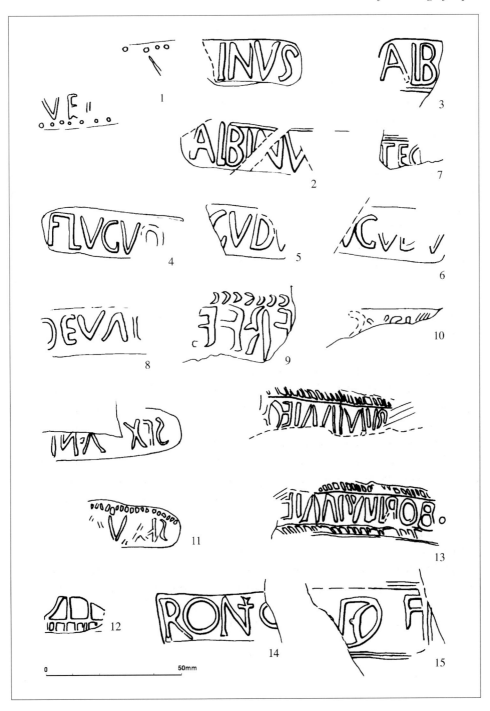

57 Mortarium stamps

from the vicinity of the headquarters building, the latter paralleled by similar discoveries from other sites, confirms that such documents would have existed. Indeed, the ink writing tablets recovered from both Carlisle and Vindolanda suggest that accounts, memoranda and reports were a regular feature of daily life on the frontier, whether recording the issue of the grain ration, the location and activities of the soldiers or the state of their weaponry. Once again, however, this is likely to have involved only relatively small numbers of the troops.

RELIGIOUS OBSERVANCE

Formal religious observance was an important part of military life, with regular dedications made to the imperial family by the garrison as a whole as part of an annual calendar of observances, as recorded in the *Feriale Duranum*, the papyrus from Dura Europos in Syria which lists the religious observances of the garrison, the *cohors XX Palmyrenorum*. The *aedes*, centrally located at the rear of the *principia*, where the imperial statues and standards of the unit were housed, was the religious focus of the fort. This was also why it often housed the unit's strong-box to provide both physical and divine protection to the unit's funds. Though there is no epigraphic or papyrological evidence from Elginhaugh to attest such religious activity, there are some hints provided by the archaeological evidence. A shallow pit containing charcoal and cremated bone in the south-east corner of the courtyard of the headquarters building may be a ritual deposit derived from a formal ceremony related to the foundation of the fort, as suggested for similar pits in broadly contemporary installations at Pen Llystyn and Inchtuthil. That such a ceremony took place is also suggested by the coin hoard deposited in the construction trench at the front of the headquarters building (above, chapter two). The unusual makeup of the hoard, with a virtually unduplicated majority of Republican issues and an odd group of imperial pieces, indicates selectivity which, combined with its location close to the exact centre of the fort, suggests that it constituted a formal foundation deposit.

The only direct evidence of more personal religious belief, however, is a steatite amulet and perhaps the fragments of Lyon ware (including a rare cup), which Steven Willis has suggested may have been used in the practice of rites or ceremonies by the officers. There is, however, no hint in the location of material in pits or elsewhere of the structured deposition which might indicate some associated religious or ritual activity, as has been suggested for the filling of a number of the pits or wells excavated within the fort and annexe at Newstead.

FOOD AND ITS PREPARATION

Food preparation and consumption, for both the troops and their mounts, would have occupied much of the men's time. According to the literary and archaeological evidence, the standard military diet consisted of corn, bacon, cheese and vegetables, but could be extremely varied. The staple was corn, by preference wheat. The military ration has been variously calculated, but a figure of 59-78lb per man/month seems to comply with Polybius, the original second-century BC Greek source on which most calculations seem to be based, with the corn dole in Rome and with the recently discovered late first-century ink writing tablet from Carlisle which lists the wheat and barley issued to the *turmae* of a cavalry *ala* for a period of three days. The importance of cereals in the diet of the troops at Elginhaugh is confirmed by a range of evidence: the quantities of carbonised wheat grains recovered during the excavation, particularly from the annexe; the size of the granaries (see *21* and *colour plate 11*), covering some 460m² and representing 4.5 per cent of the internal area of the fort within the intervallum road covered by buildings; the presence of numerous baking ovens around the perimeter of the fort; and the frequent recovery of pieces of lava quernstone from within it (below). With that said, the use of the granaries was not necessarily restricted to the storage of grain, nor the use of the ovens to the baking of bread.

The wheat would have been consumed in the form of bread, pasta, soup or porridge. Unfortunately, it was not possible to identify the wheat bran fragments recovered from several of the ditches of the fort and the well in the headquarters building to a particular species. The appearance of flax with the bran in the sample from the north ditch may suggest that the flour/cereal was used to make a gruel favoured by Roman troops. Alternatively, since a large percentage of the wheat grain identified was spelt, it may be indirect evidence that bread was produced, since spelt wheat makes better flour. The flax and other attested seeds (opium poppy, celery and dill) may have been used as flavourings. However, the presence of quantities of carbonised barley in a shallow pit cut into one of the fort ovens may indicate that it did have some role to play in feeding the garrison.

Though it is an attested element of the military diet, there is little evidence for the eating of fruit at Elginhaugh. The only finds were of imported fig from a latrine pit at the officers' end of barrack 12 (*58*) and a few examples of locally available fruits, blackberry/raspberry and sloe, the latter recovered from pits in the commanding officer's house and barrack 10, and from the grain-drying oven (498) in the annexe. Fig pips have also been recorded from a latrine pit at the officer's end of one of the contemporary barracks at Carlisle.

Though meat was certainly eaten, its role in the military diet has proved extremely difficult to quantify, a situation not helped in Scotland by the generally poor preservation of bone evidence because of the acidity of the soils. Indeed, meat may not have formed as significant a part of the diet as has often been assumed. A daily ration as high as 1.4lb per man has been postulated, based on a sixth-century AD papyrus from Egypt. But a recent calculation, based on the analysis of well-preserved faunal remains from the waterlogged auxiliary fort site at Valkenburg in the Netherlands, has suggested a figure of only 0.13lb. Though this seems rather low, it complies with the calculated daily distribution of meat in Rome in the late third century AD and, in combination with the estimated wheat ration, it would have provided sufficient sustenance for a physically active male.

58 Fig pips from the latrine in barrack 12

Analysis of the bone evidence from Britain indicates a preference for beef and pork amongst the military (approximately 70 and 20 per cent respectively), with lamb/goat making up the bulk of the remaining 10 per cent.

The evidence from Elginhaugh offers broad support for these generalisations, though little bone material was recovered from the site, and that which was retrieved was generally poorly preserved and much of it unidentifiable as to species. This was the result of both depositional and post-depositional factors, primarily the acidic nature of the soil and the fact that most of the bone had been subject to intense heat. The latter would suggest, however, that the animals had, indeed, been eaten, though there was only limited evidence of butchery marks and marrow extraction. The presence of a cheese wring (if that is the correct functional interpretation of these pottery vessels with holes in the base rather than simply a colander) perhaps indicates the consumption of other animal products. As expected, cattle were the most frequently represented amongst the identified bones. Next came horse, though the picture here is inflated by the recovery of the scattered fragments of a single skull from disturbed rampart material/demolition by the east gate. This is not to say that horse was not eaten, but in this case the remains are more likely to derive from a natural casualty, or perhaps even a ritual deposit, given the strong evidence for a cavalry garrison. Sheep/goats were also consumed on the site, but not in large quantities. The limited number of pig bones present, however, is more surprising, given that pork was also usually favoured in the military diet. Other species were rarely represented. A single bird bone was recovered in the rake-out material from one of the ovens in the south-west corner of the fort, and a single fish bone came from the flue of an oven in the annexe, though neither was identifiable as to species. However, the presence of marine molluscs is a further indication of the range of foodstuffs potentially available; oyster shells were recovered from several demolition contexts within the fort, from one metalled surface in the annexe and were frequently found across the area of the annexe during fieldwalking. Whelks were found in a lean-to structure at the rear of the rampart north of the west gate and on the surface of the adjacent intervallum road.

Olive oil and wine were essential elements of the Roman diet and are well attested, if indirectly, by the recovery of numerous fragments of amphorae. The most frequently recovered were of form Dressel 20 (between nine and twenty-five vessels are attested) (nos 4-6), which were used for the transport of olive oil from Baetica in southern Spain. But only limited numbers (two or three vessels) of western Mediterranean wine amphorae (Dressel forms 2-4, no. 1) were found (59). The relatively large numbers of flagons and beakers from the site attest the consumption of liquids, without, of course, giving any hint of their character. Some imported luxuries are also attested. As noted above, at least one of the officers had eaten figs, perhaps imported in a 'carrot amphora' as these are generally regarded as containers for dried fruit, usually dates (no. 2). It is interesting to note that the only stratified context for any of the four sherds attested is the fill of the latrine in the commanding officer's house. Some sort of fish-based product, imported from the southern Spanish coast, is indicated by the presence of probably only a single amphora of form Dressel 38 (no. 3).

Cylindrical, square and hexagonal blue-green bottle fragments represent nearly 75 per cent of the vessel glass assemblage (*60* e.g. nos 35-47). These vessels were produced as transport and household containers in many different sizes and the variation in their rim and neck diameters indicates that they contained products, ranging from the easily poured to the semi solid. Their presence points to the delivery of materials (probably foodstuffs), either as personal imports or as official supplies for the unit. Unfortunately the nature of the foodstuffs cannot be established.

Food preparation would have taken up a good deal of the soldiers' time and this activity is well attested around the fort. Ovens occurred in groups, usually of two or more, around the perimeter of the fort, though the poor preservation of some examples made precise calculation of the total number difficult. They were usually set against the back of the rampart and in some cases seem to have been slightly recessed into it. Most partly overlay the intervallum road, indicating that their construction came at the end of the building sequence within the fort. Most of the ovens were situated in the *praetentura*, matching the concentration of barrack blocks: a bank of five in the south-west corner; two pairs on either side of the south gate; a group of two or possibly three in the south-east corner; and a further possible single example just to the north of that group (*14*). Only one group of ovens was recorded in the *retentura*, a bank of two or possibly four situated against the back of the western rampart opposite the western end of barrack 2. A group of two or more might have been expected in the north-east corner, but the east side was taken up by the workshop. Any examples located at the back of the north rampart are unlikely to have survived the plough.

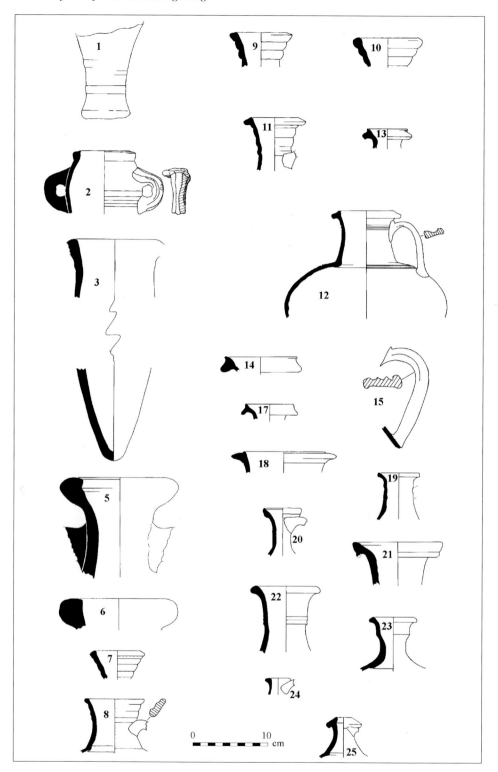

59 Coarseware amphorae (1-6) and flagon types (7-25)

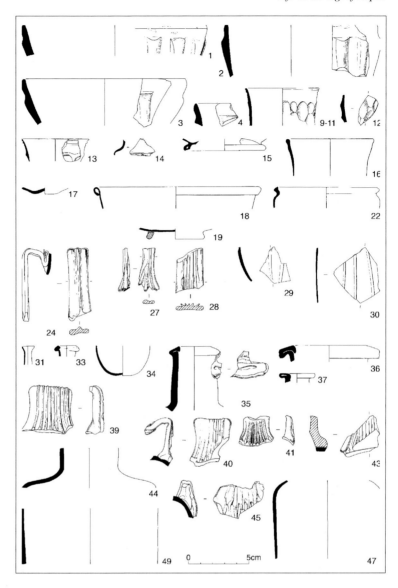

60 Glass bowls, beakers, jugs and bottles

   The best-preserved group of ovens were the four in the south-west corner (*61* and *colour plate 23*). They were circular or oval in plan, at least 1.6m and up to 2.1m in internal diameter, the larger dimensions running from front to back. A section through one well-preserved example showed that it was founded upon a cobble base, the floor being made up of clay. The outer walls were constructed from rough sandstone slabs bonded with clay. Each oven was provided with a projecting, approximately rectangular, stone platform or hob at the front, around which was a halo of ash and charcoal debris. The two central ovens faced north, while those at the east and west end of the group faced east and north-west respectively, presumably to facilitate ease of access in a relatively confined area.

The nature of the original superstructure of the ovens is uncertain. The outer walls did not survive above the level of the floor, but may have continued upwards corbelling inwards, or a dome may have been created from wattle and clay. Given the relative abundance of flat sandstone slabs in the demolition layers sealing the ovens in the south-west corner, the former seems the more likely, though the quantities of unburnt clay recovered from around the ovens to the west of the south gate would be more indicative of a clay superstructure.

These are excellent examples of the standard military cooking oven and show exactly the same location, design characteristics and range of size as the well-preserved examples from the contemporary sites at Fendoch and Inchtuthil. The ovens would have been fired by burning fuel, presumably wood, within them until the desired temperature was achieved. The burning contents were then raked out, as the mass of ash and charcoal generally found around them testifies, the bread or other items to be baked placed in the interior, and the door sealed until they were cooked. Raising the ovens up from the contemporary ground surface would have facilitated ease of operation, while the provision of a platform or hob at the front would have ensured that the cooked contents could be withdrawn with less risk of dropping them into the surrounding debris. The ovens were located at the rear of the rampart to isolate them from the timber buildings within the fort. This served both to minimise the fire risk, the intervallum road acting, in effect, as a fire break, and to keep the main area of the fort as clean as possible.

None of the ovens appeared to have been enclosed within a building or cookhouse, as is sometimes attested. A low, short and roughly constructed dry-stone wall to the north of oven 2405 (*61*) was not a substantial structural feature and was presumably intended to demarcate the cooking area, contain the material raked out from the oven and prevent it from spreading over the intervallum road. Certainly the deposits sealing this area were characterised by extensive spreads of charcoal and ashes suggesting that they were composed largely of such rake-out material and attests to the regular use of the ovens. Two approximately parallel gullies just over 0.2m deep and filled with such rake-out material were traced for a distance of some 12m running immediately to the north of this dry-stone wall cutting across the intervallum road. Though superficially resembling cart tracks, their depths, the variable distance between them and the sharpness of the turn in their course suggest that they were more probably intended to drain the area.

That the ovens were heavily used is further indicated by traces of rebuilding. An arc of sandstone fragments between the two ovens to the east of the south gate may indicate the outline of a third example that would have overlapped and, therefore, could not be contemporary. The section through one of the best-preserved ovens in the south-west corner indicated that it had probably been resurfaced. The original clay lining, baked red and partially covered with a layer of ash, was sealed beneath a subsequent cobble and purple-grey clay floor only partly oxidised to a pink/red colour, though it is just possible that this represents the remains of the collapsed superstructure.

Based upon early excavations at the auxiliary fort at Fendoch, supported by later work at the legionary base at Inchtuthil, each barrack is usually thought to have had a single communal oven within easy reach, shared between the eighty men of an infantry century.

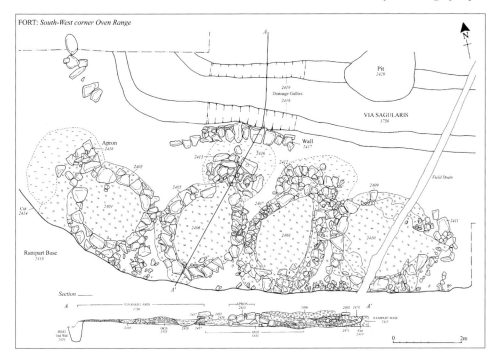

61 Detailed plan of the ovens in the south-west corner, including section through oven 2405

On this basis seven ovens might have been expected in the *praetentura* at Elginhaugh. In fact, at least ten and possibly thirteen were uncovered, making no allowance for the possibility that primary cleaning of the intervallum area failed to detect other poorly preserved examples. This would suggest that each barrack had access to more than a single oven and probably to two, bearing in mind that the two sites upon which the standard assumption is based were both excavated only very selectively. It should be noted that in the Antonine and later fort at Saalburg in Germany some nineteen ovens are known from the early excavations, somewhat in excess of the likely number of barracks within the fort. If this hypothesis is accepted, up to eight ovens would be anticipated in the *retentura* at Elginhaugh and the more limited number actually discovered is readily explained by the heavier plough damage suffered there, particularly along the eastern half of the north rampart. Given the postulated identification of the garrison as a cavalry unit, with only one *turma* in each barrack (above, chapter four), this hypothesis would indicate that some sixteen men shared each oven.

The suggestion which has sometimes been advanced that a particular concentration of ovens may be indicative of an 'official' bakery has little to commend it. It seems to be derived from the discovery of a group of three in the west corner of the fort at Pen Llystyn, but such groupings or clamps are relatively commonplace and simply reflect the convenience of concentrating such activities when possible. A bank of five ovens has been recorded near the west corner of the contemporary fort at Doune in recent excavations, and there are at least two other groups of ovens at Elginhaugh.

As the number and distribution of the ovens indicate, there was no centralised 'NAAFI' or canteen facility in Roman forts, no cooks producing food for the rest of the garrison; rather cooking was a shared, communal activity. It was probably organised by mess unit, which in an infantry unit would mean the standard *contubernium* of eight men, but given the smaller numbers of men in each *contubernium* in a cavalry *turma*, two or more *contubernia* may have cooked together. A graffito scratched before firing on a mortarium from the legionary base at Usk in south Wales indicates that it belonged to the *contubernium* of a soldier called Messor. An ink writing tablet from Carlisle contemporary with the occupation at Elginhaugh makes clear that both wheat and barley were issued to the decurion of each *turma* from central supplies, presumably in the granary, every three days for redistribution to his troop. The need to subdivide such an issue of grain between each *contubernium* may account for the presence of a very fine steelyard and its associated lead weights in the post-Roman plough soil over the officers' end of barrack 2 (*62*).

This division into small groups for both cooking and eating is further indicated by the widespread distribution of quernstone fragments across the fort, often reused in secondary cobbling. They are made from lightweight volcanic tuff, which is generally agreed to have come from Mayen near Coblenz in the Rhineland in Germany, and appear to have been a standard military issue. They are of quite distinctive design, though most of the examples from Elginhaugh were eroded and shapeless fragments because the lava is relatively soft and does not seem to survive well in the acid soils.

One or two better-preserved examples indicate that the lower stone would have had a vertical side, an irregular but hollow under surface, and a conical convex upper or grinding surface picked with radial grooves to help catch the cereal grains and improve grinding efficiency (*63*). A tall iron spindle would have been fitted into a wooden plug or bush rammed tightly into the central hole. The upper stone is more massive with a vertical side and a conical, concave grinding surface, again picked with radial grooves, which fits exactly onto the lower stone and would have been turned with an upright handle attached to its upper side.

The broken remains of the various pottery forms and, to a lesser extent, glassware were also widely distributed across the site, further indicating that both the preparation and consumption of foodstuffs was a dispersed activity. Though not an entirely consistent pattern, the distribution within the fort of samian, the fine red gloss tableware, particularly the decorated forms, tended to concentrate towards the officers' ends of the barracks, a pattern which was especially visible in barracks 2, 5-7, and 9-12. Surprisingly, the commanding officer's house has comparatively little samian, though more exotic tableware may have been used in such an equestrian household, particularly metal ware, which would have been removed when the fort was evacuated. Several pieces of copper alloy vessels were recovered, mainly from demolition deposits around the fort, but with no particular focus in the area of the commanding officer's house, and also from the annexe where at least one handle fragment looks as though it had been chopped up ready for recycling. Vessels included two shallow pans or *paterae* for cooking or serving food, the equivalent of the modern military mess tin, two plain flagon handles, possibly

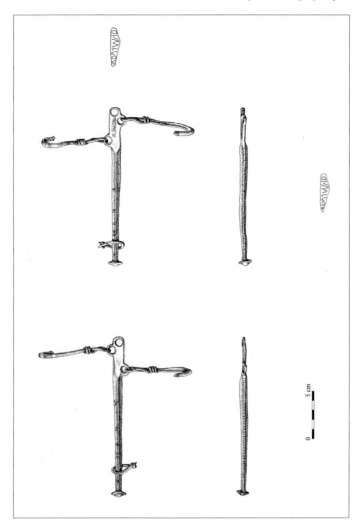

62 Copper alloy steelyard

from the same vessel, the decorated handle of a bowl and fragments of two other thin-walled bowls. Glass vessels might also have been expected to show a more significant presence in the commanding officer's quarters than they did. Perhaps greater care was exercised in keeping them scrupulously clean, with any breakages entirely removed from the area. Most of the domestic glassware comes from demolition deposits over the intervallum road in the south-west corner of the fort, though a number of vessels were found in the annexe, several from the construction trenches of buildings, and several from demolition contexts in the barracks.

Vivien Swan has suggested that one can identify a consistent pattern within military coarseware assemblages on the northern frontier which represents the standard 'issue' of a specific range of pots for a group of soldiers in a *contubernium*. At Elginhaugh coarseware jars for cooking and storage (see *56*), mortaria for pounding or mixing (see *55*) and other forms of bowl predominate, with rather lesser numbers of shallow dishes,

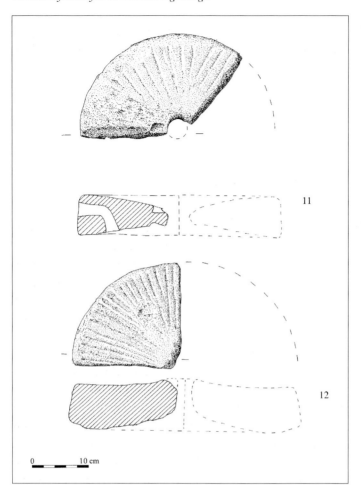

63 Roman quernstones

flagons for serving liquids, beakers and cups for drinking, and lids. Platters or dishes for serving or eating food predominate amongst the samian ware, closely followed by large decorated bowls, with slightly more limited numbers of cups. Similarly, a good range, if more limited numbers, of glass tableware for drinking and serving food and drink was found, mainly bowls, drinking vessels and jars or jugs (see *60*).

Finally, the Romans recognised that a plentiful water supply was essential for any garrison, all the more so if, as at Elginhaugh, there were horses involved. The location of a fort at a river crossing would have served a practical as well as strategic function, for the horses could have been readily watered by the river. For the men, however, a purer supply was needed and it has been calculated that each soldier required some 2.5l of water per day for drinking and cooking. Forts occupied over a long period of time might be provided with an aqueduct, but more usually a well was dug, almost always in the courtyard of the headquarters building – so too at Elginhaugh where a well was located in the north-east corner. It was 1.8m deep and had been lined with wattles made from hazel and alder (*colour plate 13*). The construction shaft for the well was some 2.5m in diameter and had been packed with quite stony material, particularly towards the top, to provide additional revetting of the unstable sandy soil through which it was dug. Three small post holes formed a triangle with the well at its centre and probably supported the legs of a tripod which would have housed some form of lifting mechanism (see *18*). Three other wells of similar design were dug after the buildings within the fort were demolished and relate to its subsequent use as a collection centre for animals (below, chapter seven).

HEALTH AND WELFARE

When not on active duty, eating or sleeping, the troops may have passed some time at their leisure. By the later first century AD all Roman military installations were provided with a bathhouse, which may have been a focus for such activity, though this may have been only a relatively recent development in relation to auxiliary forts, for Elginhaugh is one of only two examples known in Flavian Scotland, the other being at Newstead, a large fort whose garrison at this time is uncertain and may have included a legionary presence. Auxiliary bathhouses were usually, but not always, located outside the defences. At Elginhaugh the bathhouse lies not within the annexe, but on an almost imperceptible shelf, aligned along the contour, on what now seems totally unsuitable, steeply-sloping ground some 20m below the level of the fort and 10m above the floodplain of the River North Esk. The aerial photograph indicated that it was divided it into three rooms with an 'apsidal' projection at the western end (see *2*). Brief trial excavation and probing by Gordon Maxwell indicated that it was constructed on neatly-coursed, clay-mortared walls on stout clay-and-cobble foundations and measured about 19.2m x 7.5m (excluding the 'apsidal' projection) (*64*). The inner face of the north wall at the north-west corner stood to a height of over 1.1m in eleven courses and the outer was even higher. Two brick-built pillars, each consisting of three square bricks on a bipartite tile plinth, and traces of *opus signinum* (a waterproof mixture of concrete and tile) from the flooring indicated the presence of a hypocaust. This western room was presumably the *caldarium* or hot room; the middle room the *tepidarium* or warm room; and the third room the *frigidarium* or cold room. The projection at the western end is best interpreted as the cheeks of the stokehole to heat the *caldarium*. A faint parchmark running parallel to the bathhouse and about 7m north of its eastern half just visible in some air photographs may indicate the location of a dressing room (*apodyterium*). Similarly, immediately to the south of the westernmost room at an angle of approximately 35° to the south wall, parchmarks appear to define a roughly rectangular stone-built structure, possibly a latrine, from which a drain curved away downslope.

Bathing was an important part of daily routine in Roman society. It was a communal activity, conducted in facilities that have much in common with modern spas or Turkish baths. Apart from their normal hygienic functions, the baths provided facilities for exercise, recreation and social interaction, all important in helping to foster the bonding and spirit of unity so vital to the efficient functioning of a military unit.

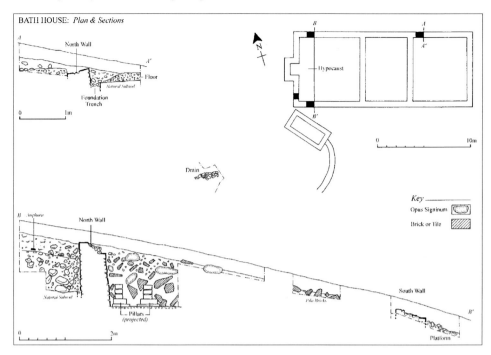

64 Plan of the bathhouse and section across its western end

As noted above (chapter four), the bath building is large, perhaps a reflection of the higher status of cavalry amongst auxiliary units, but the excavation was insufficiently extensive to provide any detailed evidence of the nature of the activities which would have taken place within it. In the fort itself, however, several counters or gaming pieces, mainly black or white glass, were found in a number of locations, perhaps hinting at the widespread use of board games.

The bathhouse may also have provided the communal latrine for the troops, if the parchmark visible from the air has been correctly identified, the effluent draining away down the hill. Latrines are not uncommonly associated with bathhouses because both involved the management of copious amounts of water. But some officers were provided with their own private latrines within the fort. Thus the commanding officer and his family seem to have had some form of earth closet latrine at the rear of the accommodation (above, chapter three) (*colour plate 19*) and at least one and probably two groups of officers were also provided with latrines at their end of their barrack blocks (11 and 12) (see *31*). The latrine pit in barrack 12 consisted of two circular pits, one inside and one outside the building, connected together towards the top by a gully that cut through the construction trench of the end wall of the barrack. The deeper, outer pit would appear to have functioned as a soakaway, the connecting gully facilitating overflow out under the barrack wall in the manner of the modern U-bend (*65*). Its identification as a latrine was supported by the presence in the primary waterlogged silt fill of the outer pit of large quantities of fig seeds (see *58*), which would appear to have passed through the

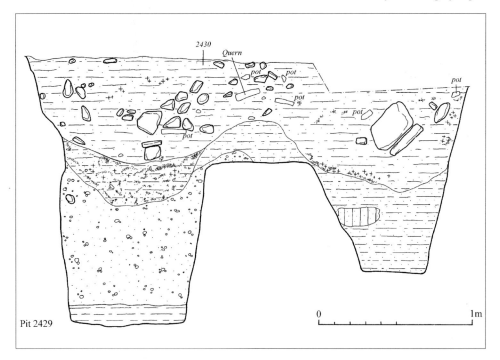

2430
Quern
pot
pot
pot
pot
pot
pot
pot

Pit 2429

0   1m

65 Section through the latrine pits in barrack 12

human digestive tract. A similar arrangement, with the latrine inside the officer's quarters and the cesspit outside connected by a channel through the wall, was recorded in barrack I at Hod Hill. There is some uncertainty about whether or not the outer pit had been covered. If it were not, it would certainly have interfered with passage around the *via sagularis* and the operation of the nearby cooking ovens, though the presence of an intersecting drainage gully (2419) cut into the intervallum road immediately outside the barrack wall is likely to have affected its efficient operation (see *61*). Either some form of wooden covering had collapsed, accounting for an accumulation of demolition deposits in the upper filling, or the outer pit was a later addition to the latrine, cutting through the drainage gully, and had been left open. This sequence of events would also account for the need to provide a second gully mirroring the first, but positioned nearer to the ovens. A pit in barrack II, though smaller and more elongated, had similar characteristics: it was in the same general position in relation to the officers' quarters, though in a rear room rather than at the front; it straddled the end wall of the block; and was slightly deeper on the outside of the building. However, it was not deep enough to be waterlogged and no organic remains were found to confirm its identification as a latrine.

The Roman army was also aware of the need to ensure that reasonable conditions were maintained underfoot, though at Elginhaugh there is also a link between drainage of surface water and latrines. The two elements were linked at the rear of the commanding officer's house where a pit (III), into which it seems likely that the contents of the commanding officer's earth closet latrine were deposited, had been

66 T-junction in the drain at the rear of the west gate, partially disturbed by the second phase of post hole 2095

provided with a stone-lined overflow drain. This curved away under the intervallum road to the north-west and fed into the main drain running along the back of the rampart (see *52*). Moreover, analysis of the macroplant remains hinted at the possible presence of cess in both the inner north and east ditches. In laying the drains to discharge any outflow into the fort ditches, as is clearly attested at all four gates, the builders of Elginhaugh were following normal practice. Examination of the outer ditch of the annexe at the Antonine fort at Bearsden indicated that it was full of cess channelled out from an adjacent latrine.

Timber-lined drains are presumed to have been the norm in the timber-built Flavian forts in northern Britain. They survive all too rarely, though excellent examples have been uncovered as a result of the waterlogged condition of the remains at Carlisle (*colour plate 16*) and Vindolanda. Most of the drains within the fort at Elginhaugh, however, were constructed of rough sandstone slabs forming a channel some 0.25-0.4m sq internally, the basal slabs set in purple clay (*66*). The provision of stone-lined drains in an otherwise timber-built fort is rather unusual; even the legionary fortress at Inchtuthil was only partly provided with stone-lined drains. It may indicate some recognition that drainage might be a problem on the site, or may be related to a recognition of the additional drainage requirements of a cavalry unit whose horses were stabled with the men.

The fort was reasonably well served by drains, though the complete system was not uncovered (*67*). Clearly, given the number of times the north wall of barrack 3 had been repaired, the major drainage problem during occupation of the fort was in the north-

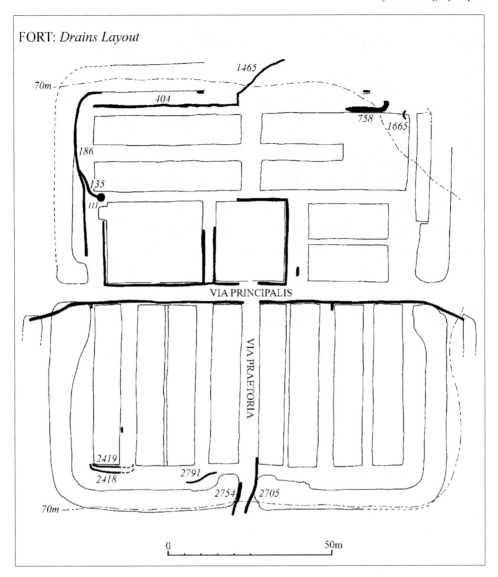

FORT: *Drains Layout*

67 The pattern of drains within the fort

east corner. Ironically, that area seems originally to have been relatively ill provided with drains, though more may have been lost to the plough. The main focus of the drainage system seems to have been the central range of buildings, particularly the headquarters building and commanding officer's house. Drains ran around three sides of the latter and probably entirely surrounded the former, further emphasising their importance, though it is not clear exactly how these led water away from the buildings because other elements of the system were not traced or did not survive the plough.

Drains ran east and west along the south side of the *via principalis* from either side of the *via praetoria*, draining out through the east and west gates, following the edge of the rampart and issuing into the inner ditch. This provision drained the northern ends of all the barrack blocks in the *praetentura*, though at only one point, on the west side of barrack 6, was there any sign of a connecting drain running alongside any of those barracks. In addition, one fragment of drain was recorded alongside the officers' quarters on the eastern side of barrack 12, though this is more likely to have drained to the south, perhaps linking into one of the open gullies at the south end of that block. A T-junction identified in the drain at the rear of the west gate suggests that that there may have been some provision for drainage along the back of the rampart opposite barrack 12 (*66*). It is uncertain how long-lasting or effective these arrangements to drain the *praetentura* were, since the drain through the east gate was cut away by a deep slot which blocked the gate and was not subsequently reinstated, while that through the west gate seems to have been cut away by a post pit of phase 2. A drain also ran out through the east side of the south gate, apparently originating by the south-west corner of building 8. A second apparently unlined drain starting by the threshold of the same gate on the west side of the road must originally have been lined with timber if it was to work at all.

Drainage provision in the north-west corner of the fort was slightly more complex. An apparently unlined drainage gully ran around the outer edge of the intervallum road, starting just to the north of the west gate, and was joined by a stone-lined overflow channel from a large cess pit located at the rear of the commanding officer's house, before continuing towards the inner corner of the rampart. Thereafter its course becomes uncertain, though it may eventually have connected with a gully issuing out of the north gate.

Secondary and more localised open drains were constructed at several points to combat particular problems, such as the large drainage gully intended to drain water away from the adjacent wall of barrack 3 and the double line of U-shaped gullies located to ensure that the bank of ovens in the south-west corner remained dry.

Care of the sick and wounded is an important provision for any army and it is sometimes suggested that Roman forts were each provided with their own hospital. While this can be asserted with some confidence in relation to legionary fortresses, their identification in auxiliary forts is not without dispute; some buildings so identified are more likely to have been workshops and no auxiliary hospital has been indisputably identified. However, auxiliary *medici* (physicians or medical orderlies) are known from inscriptions and one of the Vindolanda tablets refers to soldiers at the hospital. There is no direct evidence of a hospital building at Elginhaugh, though there are a few finds which may hint at medical provision in the fort. Several artefacts may have been medical instruments (*68*), including a copper alloy shaft which has lost its ends (no. 57), two hollow rods (nos 58 and 74), a handle (no. 148) and a narrow strip of iron with parallel sides and a loose rectangular loop of copper alloy encircling the shank which represents the arm and hinge of a pair of iron tweezers. Such tweezers are unusual finds in forts, since they tend to be more associated with female toilet activities, and the restraining ring is more often a feature of medical forceps than domestic tweezers. There are also two small pale blue-green glass bottles that are usually interpreted as unguent or cosmetic containers (*60*, no. 31), but which may also have been used for medical preparations.

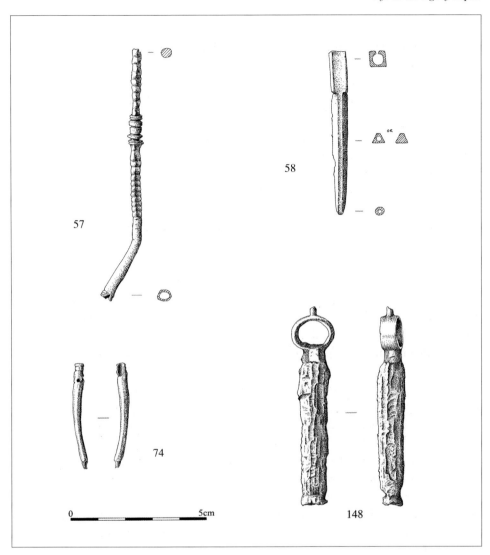

57

58

74

148

0   5cm

68 Possible medical instruments

QUALITY OF LIFE AND SOCIAL DIFFERENTIATION

The overall impression gained from the striking range and wealth of the artefactual material recovered from the site is of a relatively wealthy consumer society with access to a wide range of goods from far and wide. Despite its location close to the northern limit of Roman occupation and relatively short period of occupation, the occupants of the fort enjoyed a considerable range of creature comforts associated with the classical lifestyle, ranging from imported wine, olive oil and figs, through fine samian tableware and glass vessels, to elaborate pieces of furniture. With that said, there are, as one would expect in a hierarchical military system, clear indications of social differentiation in the

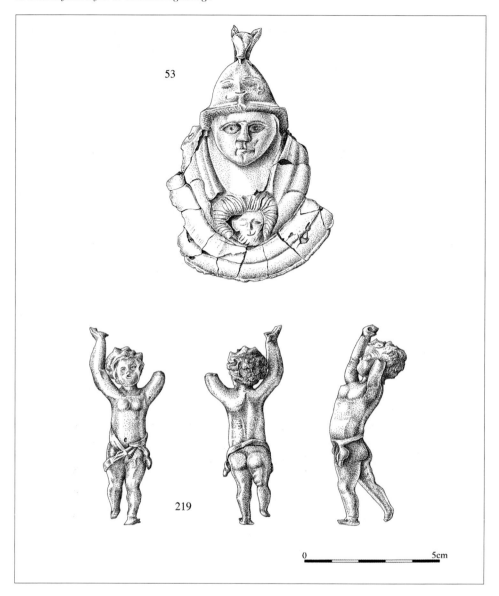

69 Furniture fittings

accommodation provided and in the distribution of some of the artefactual material, even if the latter has been somewhat masked by the demolition process during which rubbish was collected together and burnt.

The commanding officer's house with its internal courtyard or peristyle arrangement is basically a Mediterranean design for the town house of a relatively wealthy family. Indeed, the commanding officer would have been accompanied by his family and servants. The presence of the former is hinted at by the single examples of a woman's *calceus* shoe from the well in the headquarters building and a child's shoe from the inner east ditch (see *49*, nos 1 and 3). Something of the nature of life on the northern frontier for the commanding officer and his family is indicated by the broadly contemporary ink tablets from Vindolanda which include the correspondence between two such auxiliary officers and their wives, most famous of which is the invitation to Sulpicia Lepidina, wife of the commanding officer of the 9th Cohort of Batavians stationed at Vindolanda, from her friend Claudia Severa, wife of another auxiliary prefect stationed nearby, to her birthday party.

The size of the commanding officer's house, by far the largest building in the fort, and its architectural pretensions are entirely appropriate for the commanding officer of an auxiliary cavalry unit, a man of equestrian rank and, therefore, of considerable social standing within Roman society. It is extremely likely that the windows in the building would have been glazed, since every other Flavian fort in the northern frontier region with a substantial group of glass finds has produced at least one piece of window glass, though surprisingly none was recovered from Elginhaugh. One or two artefacts do, however, give indications of the wealth of the internal furnishings (*69*). Thus a large hollow copper alloy mount in the form of a helmeted bust of Minerva from the fill of a post-fort gully just across the road from the commanding officer's house would appear to be a decorative element from a large item of furniture, such as a couch or a table, though perhaps of provincial manufacture. While a small, well made lead figurine of a rather chubby naked child, with a piece of cloth loosely tied around his waist and his hands held above his head, was possibly a support for a tray, bowl or lamp and probably not the product of a provincial workshop.

Similar social or rank differentiation is apparent in the architecture of the barrack blocks. While three troopers shared a simple single room at the rear of the barracks, covering no more than 14m², the quarters for the officers took up some 22.5-25.2 per cent of each block, the actual surface area varying between 84m² and 98m², while the officers' quarters in the double barrack (3 and 4) covered a massive 437m² (above, chapter four and *Table 1*). Even if the decurion was sharing the accommodation with his two under officers, the *principales*, and seven horses, that still represents a provision of personal accommodation four times greater than that for each trooper. The officers' quarters are further distinguished by their subdivision into a range of rooms, with no two blocks exactly the same, though each broadly based on three rooms on either side of the central wall, and the provision in some cases of additional features such as storage pits and latrines. At least one latrine pit is known from the officer's end of the contemporary barracks at Carlisle. There was also a tendency, as noted above, for the distribution of the fine red gloss samian tableware to concentrate at the officers' end of the block.

SEVEN

IMPACT AND INTERACTION

LOCAL ENVIRONMENT AND PRE–ROMAN SETTLEMENT

The gently sloping terrace overlooking the river North Esk on which the fort at Elginhaugh is situated seems to have been an attractive location for settlement for almost as long as man is known to have been active in Scotland, despite the occasional drainage problems likely to have been caused by the high clay and silt content of the underlying deposits. Occupation of Mesolithic date involving flint knapping was attested in the centre of the field beneath the western rampart of the fort – Neolithic activity took the form of shallow pits containing quantities of pottery sealed beneath the intervallum road adjacent to the east rampart of the fort, while an early Bronze Age presence was indicated by remains of two pits containing beaker pottery in the annexe, one in trench 9 and the other beneath the road in trench 3. Evidence of cultivation of the soil by ard at some unspecified time prior to the Roman arrival was also attested in the vicinity of, but later than, the Neolithic (*70*) pits and part of a post hole defined round house was revealed in annexe trench 7, also undated but probably of later Bronze Age or early Iron Age date.

Ironically, evidence of the anticipated Iron Age occupation site, which trial trenching by Gordon Maxwell in 1979 had suggested would be present, was not forthcoming. Given the recovery of Iron Age pottery from what was interpreted as a construction trench underlying part of what subsequently proved to be the commanding officer's house, particular attention was paid to the linear features that were detected beneath it and the headquarters building. Careful examination made clear, however, that they were of geological rather than archaeological significance. When plotted they made no coherent, regular pattern; they were filled primarily with sand and gravel; and, where sectioned, they proved to be up to 1m deep, irregular in profile, narrowing rapidly from a width of *c* 0.5m to 0.05m. Traces of one were also recorded sealed beneath a metalled surface in the annexe associated with a pit of late Neolithic/early Bronze Age date. Such features are, therefore, most likely to have been ice wedges.

Indeed, the general impression gained during the excavation was of a lack of structures on the site immediately prior to the construction of the Roman fort. Surviving turf lines beneath the ramparts and roads at several points indicate that, prior to the building of

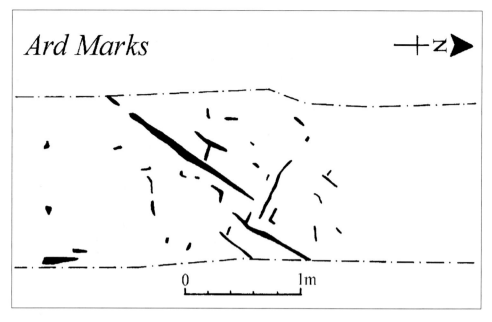

70 Ard marks cutting the old ground surface beneath the intervallum road north of barrack 3

the fort, the site was under pasture. The same picture is provided by the pollen analysis. The relatively low herb pollen values and the absence of heather indicate well-grazed grassland in the immediate vicinity of the fort. The macrofossil evidence offers further refinement, indicating a mosaic of different types of grassland according to variations in the local soil conditions, including damper rushy areas, more acidic patches of heath grass and areas of short turf. Though small quantities of late Bronze Age and Iron Age pottery were recovered from various locations across both fort and annexe, they were always in secondary or disturbed contexts, and their distribution across the site might reasonably be explained as the result of past manuring. The aerial photographic evidence suggests the presence of settlements potentially of later prehistoric date only a few hundred metres away to the east, including a defended enclosure probably of Iron Age date and a palisaded enclosure (see 3). In addition, excavation has confirmed the Iron Age date of a pit alignment, a form of land division, across the river to the south and an unenclosed house and nearby palisaded enclosure some 0.5km to the west.

This evidence indicates that the fort was imposed within, if not directly upon, an area of pre-existing settlement, though this makes it difficult to estimate the impact on the local settlement pattern. Clearly the construction of the fort did not involve the displacement of settlement on the site itself, but it seems unlikely that the nearby defended enclosure, if still occupied, would have been allowed so to continue. On the other hand, there is no reason to postulate the general clearance of settlement in the area. Excavations on two broadly contemporary Iron Age settlement enclosures at Port Seton, located some 12km to the north-east of Elginhaugh overlooking the Firth of Forth, indicate that although one went out of use in the late first century AD, the other continued to be occupied, while extensive aerial survey and more limited excavation elsewhere in the region in recent decades has indicated a considerable density of settlements of later Iron Age date apparently largely unaffected by the Roman presence.

A further important question is the nature and extent of the associated cultivated landscape. What is clear is that there was only limited woodland cover of a fairly restricted type in the immediate vicinity. The pollen evidence suggests alder with possibly willow on damper ground, with some hazel scrub elsewhere, a pattern broadly replicated in near contemporary analyses from the Iron Age pit alignment less than 1km away. The main components of what would normally be regarded as the natural woodland in the area, oak and birch, are notable by their absence. The charcoal identifications and surviving waterlogged wood offer the same picture with slight refinements. The consistent feature is the dominance of alder. It was the most common charcoal identified, the structural timber most frequently used and the species represented most often amongst off-cuts, twigs and branches from waterlogged contexts.

Accepting the general principle that wood employed on the site was likely to be of local origin, as the choice of alder for major structural uprights indicates (chapter three), the waterlogged samples and charcoal identification serve to refine the picture of local woodland provided by the pollen analysis. Birch, hazel and hawthorn were quite commonly identified as charcoals, with lesser amounts of oak and only two examples of willow. Among the waterlogged remains, oak and hazel were the most strongly represented after alder, hazel being the first choice for wattle and oak represented by a number of structural elements and off-cuts. A similar pattern is apparent from structures in the second century civil settlement (*vicus*) outside the fort at Inveresk some 5km to the north, where the main species employed were alder, birch and hazel, with a little oak. There was no direct indication of either hazel or alder stems being derived from formally coppiced woodland, though particular age concentrations did suggest that suitable stands were being irregularly cut over. In summary, therefore, the evidence indicates the presence of alder carr, probably along the River Esk, containing both fully-grown mature trees and irregularly cut stools. On limited areas of dry ground, similar stools of hazel will have predominated with occasional oak or birch trees. Thus, the Roman army may have needed to forage slightly further afield to meet all their building requirements. The Stracathro-gated camp at Woodhead, some 7km to the south-west, has been linked with that process, its attached *c.*10ha enclosure possibly acting as a storage compound for timber felled for the construction of the fort at Elginhaugh. Thus, the Roman impact on the remaining sparse woodland cover, and particularly on the availability of mature trees, would have been substantial.

The combined evidence from the different modes of analysis is less clear on the question of the extent of arable cultivation in the vicinity of the fort. The pollen record provides little certain evidence for cereal cultivation contemporary with occupation of the fort. This is consistent with the pattern recorded from Roman forts elsewhere in Lowland Scotland of extensive grazed pasture land with only hints of arable cultivation, usually of barley. Very small amounts of barley are represented in the pollen record at Elginhaugh, but these might be explained by the difficulty of distinguishing cultivated barley pollen from some wild grasses of the same group, or the presence of pollen attached to barley bran fragments in the ditch deposit concerned, though the poor representation of cereals in the pollen record generally makes interpretation of the significance of small amounts more difficult.

However, this implied emphasis on pastoral agriculture in the region is increasingly being contradicted by the archaeological evidence of later prehistoric arable cultivation. Plough marks are regularly discovered preserved beneath the ramparts of Roman forts, as for example at Cramond and Elginhaugh itself. Remains of narrow or cord rig cultivation in later prehistoric contexts have been widely recorded, particularly in the Borders, even in what are now environmentally unsuitable locations. Quernstones are common finds on Iron Age and Romano-British settlement sites in north Britain, and several Iron Age quernstones were recovered from Elginhaugh, including two partly embedded in the makeup of the intervallum road by the east gate. Finally, excavations on two broadly contemporary Iron Age settlement enclosures at Port Seton, located some 12km to the north-east of Elginhaugh overlooking the Firth of Forth, indicate the importance of cereal cultivation in their local economy (below). While the density of settlements of later Iron Age date revealed by aerial survey noted above emphasises the extent to which the landscape was being exploited agriculturally. It seems likely, therefore, that the role of arable agriculture in the surrounding area is under-represented in the pollen diagrams for a number of technical reasons, particularly the rapid fall-off rate in the dispersal of cereal pollen.

FOOD SUPPLY

Assuming that the garrison was entirely cavalry and consisted of some ten *turmae*, with one slightly enlarged, that would give a total of some 342 men (above, chapter four) and approximately 385 horses, allowing for remounts for the officers. Assuming a wheat ration of between 59 and 78lbs per man/month (above, chapter six), that would translate into 108-143 tons of wheat per annum for the whole garrison. The contemporary ink writing tablet from Carlisle, which lists the wheat and barley issued to the *turmae* of a cavalry *ala* for a period of three days, implies a ration of approximately 132lbs of barley per horse per month, which would translate into 272 tons per annum for the whole garrison. Using calculations based on the meat consumption figures of *c*.0.13lbs per man per day from Valkenburg (above, chapter six), estimates of attested military meat preferences calculated by Tony King from the bone evidence and the estimated dressed weight of carcasses, it can be estimated that the most likely garrison at Elginhaugh of some 342 men would have required only some 27-38 cattle, 65 pigs and 65-195 sheep per annum.

The general assumption should be that the army would have obtained its food supplies locally whenever possible so as to minimise any problems which might arise from overdependence on long distance transport. The difficulty lies in demonstrating the extent to which local supply was relied upon. In some instances it is clear that food was imported into the fort at Elginhaugh over considerable distances; wine and olive oil amphorae are attested, as well as figs (above, chapter six), though the quantities involved are relatively small. But for the bulk of the foodstuffs the evidence is less clear-cut.

It remains particularly problematic whether the demand for wheat could have been met locally, particularly spelt or bread wheat, which seems to have been the Roman military preference, as attested by analyses from Caerleon, York and South Shields. It has already been established (above) that arable cultivation was probably more widespread than previously assumed, but the record of macrofossil plant remains from native sites in Scotland indicates an emphasis on barley cultivation. Wheat is occasionally attested, but only as a relatively minor part of the plant assemblage, as for example from sites in Dumfriesshire and northern Northumberland. Barley also dominated the cereal assemblage at Port Seton only some 12km away and though wheat made up a substantive proportion of the cereal crops recorded, it was mainly emmer with limited amounts of spelt appearing in the early centuries AD. This largely negative evidence for suitable wheat cultivation has prompted the view that the Roman dietary preference is unlikely to have been readily met in Lowland Scotland. Indeed, the need to supply wheat may serve to explain the indications in the literary sources that grain was, indeed, shipped north for military consumption. Tacitus implies that grain requisitioned in the civil province was sometimes sent to garrisons on the frontier, while the existence of two places in the north named *Horrea Classis* (granaries of the fleet) is strongly suggestive of an established system of trans-shipping grain supplies.

Despite this more generalised pattern, there are strong indications that a reasonable proportion of the supply of grain to Elginhaugh for both human and animal consumption may have been met locally. The provision of grain driers within the annexe implies the processing of local supplies, since grain is unlikely to have been transported damp for long distances because this would have resulted in an increased rate of spoilage. A range of species was represented in the best-attested grain drier (above, chapter five) including both emmer and spelt wheats, as well as barley and some oats. It may be of significance that this provision was deemed necessary only for the first few years of the occupation of the fort during the early stages of establishing its supply system, although the presence of quantities of unprocessed or partly processed wheat and barley deposited in demolition pits on the site of barracks 1, 5 and 7 may indicate that the practice of local supply continued. Analogous evidence, though of later date, comes from South Shields and Caernarvon where specific weed species associated with the spelt wheat remains recovered from the forts were characteristic of locally grown crops. Finally, the cereal species composition itself seems to have been influenced by what was locally available. The dominant species recorded in the fort is barley, predominantly of the hulled variety, reflecting the provision of feed for the cavalry horses, though wheat still makes up almost 30 per cent of the assemblage. Proportions are almost reversed in the annexe, with wheat constituting over 75 per cent of the assemblage. The dominant wheat species in the fort is spelt, with emmer and spelt equally represented in the annexe. Bread wheat is recorded, but not in great quantities. It may not be a coincidence that barley and emmer wheat dominated the assemblages at the contemporary Iron Age settlement enclosures at Port Seton, as noted above, with spelt a late introduction. Indeed, it has been noted that emmer wheat is recorded with certainty on Roman military sites only in Scotland. It would seem not unreasonable to suggest, therefore, that the bulk of the barley requirements of the garrison would have been obtained locally as far as possible, but most of the wheat would have been imported from further south.

Though there is only limited positive evidence to support the assertion, there is no reason to believe that the meat requirements of the garrison at Elginhaugh could not have been supplied locally. The pollen evidence attests that the grassland in the area was well grazed and the more limited consumption of pork recorded in the bone evidence may indicate a greater reliance on animals which were available locally. The fact that the use of the site after the demolition of the fort involved the collection of animals (see below) would suggest that they were available in reasonable quantity. Finally, the consumption of marine molluscs noted above is a further indication of the exploitation of local resources, since such perishable foodstuffs are unlikely to have travelled far and Elginhaugh lies less than 6km from the coast.

Estimating the impact of obtaining locally the full barley requirement calculated above requires that it be translated into a percentage of local production figures, which in turn requires knowledge of both the annual yield per acre and the number of acres under cultivation. The latter figures can at best only be guessed at and would in any case vary according to local circumstances. But assuming yield figures of approximately a ton per acre, representing only two thirds of those attested in eastern Scotland in the 1950s, the area necessary to produce the barley required would have been of the order of 272 acres. This in turn represents the product of less than 3.5 per cent of the 8040 acres of land within a 2-mile (3.2km) radius of the site. The annual requisition or purchase of the product of such an area does not seem excessive for the more fertile parts of eastern Scotland and may have served to stimulate the local economy to produce a surplus, were they not already doing so. It may have also encouraged them to take advantage of the Roman market, perhaps by attempting to grow more wheat, as appears to have occurred during the Roman occupation of the Netherlands and may be indicated at Port Seton. Certainly, the presence of quantities of Roman goods on native sites, perhaps best attested in the case of Traprain Law near Haddington in East Lothian only 27km away, suggests that such trade was indeed taking place.

To what extent it was standard Roman practice to confiscate large areas of land around forts for military use is uncertain and the nature of the control over any such lands is much disputed. The presence of military land (*territorium* or *prata*) is certainly attested epigraphically in various parts of the Roman Empire, though it is usually associated with legionary fortresses. If such confiscations were commonplace in relation to all types of military establishment, the potential detrimental impact of the military presence at Elginhaugh on the local economy could have been considerable, depending upon the size of the area confiscated and whether or not the indigenous occupants were cleared from it. On the other hand, the clustering of native settlements attested around forts in north-west England would suggest that the local population retained use of the land even if it was in military ownership. Indeed, once the conquest had been completed it was in Rome's interest to maximise the economic return from taxation (below), while a general principle of minimal interference was always preferred. Neither of these requirements is compatible with any major disruption of local settlement.

POST–FORT USE OF THE SITE

One of the most unusual and unexpected aspects of the excavation was the recovery of evidence of Roman activity on the site after the demolition of the fort. Though somewhat scattered and fragmentary, the pattern is consistent. Additional cobbles or heavy metalling overlay the foundations of a number of buildings, including the commanding officer's house, one of the granaries and barracks 2, 3, 5, 6, 9, 11 and 12 (e.g. *71*), and sealed demolition material over the road through the east gate. The cobbling seems to indicate a widening of the roads within the fort, though it may simply have been better preserved at these points because of the protection from plough damage afforded by the adjacent mass of the well-constructed roads. That this was the case is hinted at by better preservation where cobbling overlay and had partly sunk into larger pits, as occurred at both the front and the back of the commanding officer's house (*72*). Thus, after the buildings were removed, it would appear that much of the internal area of the fort may have been cobbled over.

There were no signs of internal buildings contemporary with this phase, other than possibly the workshop set into the back of the rampart. This may have continued in use for smithing, for a layer rich in iron, resulting in the formation of concretion deposits, overlay the later cobbling in the north-east corner of the fort. However, the south-west quadrant seems to have been separated off from the rest of the interior by a U-shaped gully some 3m wide and 0.6m deep. This ran along the south side of the *via principalis* from the middle of barrack 9 to the east side of barrack 11, continued after a gap of 6.0m by a similar but shorter feature across barrack 12. The gully cut through demolition spreads, removed virtually all trace of the first partition wall in barracks 9, 10 and 12, and even cut through the metalling of the alleys between the blocks (see *30* and *31*). Clearly, therefore, this was not simply a demolition feature, though it contained redeposited demolition debris in its lower fill. The upper filling of the gully, particularly towards the centre, was predominantly clean grey silty clay, which suggests that it had accumulated more gradually.

The only signs of activity within the demarcated area were several temporary cooking ovens. One was located on the intervallum road at the back of the west rampart adjacent to the west-south-west interval tower (*colour plate 24*). It consisted of an oval, or rather kidney-shaped shallow depression, of which the western end served as a stokehole, with the flue or body of the oven to the east constructed of re-used tiles, voussoir bricks from the demolished bathhouse and quernstone fragments. The stokehole was filled with wood ash, charcoal, carbonised cereals and burnt bone. A further two pairs of ovens were located near the centre of the fort, overlying the northern end of barrack 9. The better-preserved pair had almost rectangular flues formed on three sides by slabs of clay

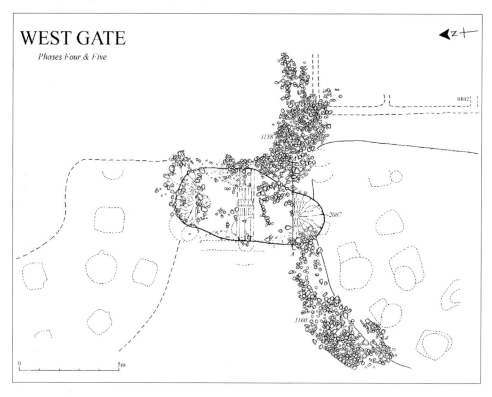

71 Plan of the west gate: phases 4 and 5

set within an irregular dump of clay up to 0.3m deep (*73*). The fourth side of each oven was open, facing west or north-west onto the common stokehole, a shallow irregular hollow. Large quantities of charcoal and further pieces of fired clay slabs were removed from their interiors, the latter presumably derived from the collapsed roof of the ovens which are likely to have been flat.

Though clearly different, these post-fort ovens were simpler, less permanent versions of the standard cooking ovens found within forts. They have rather more in common with the ovens sometimes found within temporary camps, which tend to be at least partially sunk into the ground. Broadly similar examples are known from Kintore, in Grampian, Carronbridge in Dumfriesshire, Monktonhall, Midlothian and only 0.5km away at Melville Nurseries, the first two of which contained carbonised grain. They presumably functioned as cooking ovens for whatever detachment subsequently utilised the fort enclosure, for a few wheat grains and a fragment of calcined cattle bone were recovered from one. The presence within its fill of large quantities of carbonised barley and weed species indicates the presence of locally grown animal feed grain, though whether the oven was being used to dry the cereals is unclear.

The remainder of the fort seems to have been left open, but three new wells were dug in the eastern half, which were clearly not contemporary with the buildings in the fort and the well in the headquarters building may also have continued in use. Two wells were

72 Cobbling sealing pits 1091 and 1094 at the front of the commanding officer's house (*praetorium*)

located rather too close to granary 2 to have been in contemporary use without posing potential structural hazards and the construction pit for one of them partly overlay a construction trench and one intermediate granary post pit (see *21*). One of the wells was only partially examined because it had been disturbed by a modern borehole, part of the assessment of the site by Scottish Development Agency. Removal of the first 0.5m of filling revealed a circle of cobbles 2.0m wide similar to that in the second well, which was more thoroughly investigated. Here the cobble lining was well preserved and found to have been rammed into the sides of the construction pit, roughly coursed to form a solid revetment for the inner shaft. The water table restricted conventional excavation below 1.3m without recourse to pumps and extensive shoring, so to save time, once the excavation of the immediately surrounding area had been completed, a large box of soil was removed by machine to act as a sump leaving the remains of the well upstanding in the centre. This drastic technique allowed excavation to a depth of 2.2m. Approximately 0.8m of the wattle lining of the shaft survived, identical in construction, but not so well preserved, as that in the well in the *principia*. The withies were mainly hazel with some alder; the sails largely oak with hazel and alder again. Samples were taken for botanical analysis from the upper fills suggests that the well may have been contaminated with the dumping of the products of crop processing. Though both wheat and barley were represented, the latter seems to have been the more important crop.

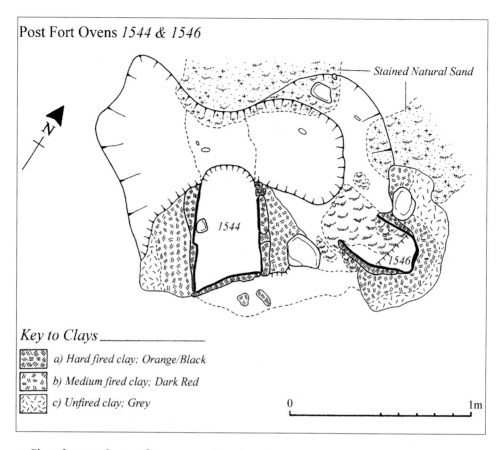

Post Fort Ovens *1544 & 1546*

Stained Natural Sand

1544

1546

Key to Clays

a) *Hard fired clay; Orange/Black*

b) *Medium fired clay; Dark Red*

c) *Unfired clay; Grey*

0   1m

73 Plan of rectangular post-fort ovens overlying barrack 9

A third well was dug through the northern end of barrack 5, its construction pit cutting the construction trench of the partition wall of the first *contubernium* and also its associated demolition pit (see *29*). The water table was encountered at a depth of just under a metre and the sides of the excavation began to collapse from the constant inflow of water. Thus, once the other features in the area had been examined, the area around the well was lowered by machine to provide a sump leaving the remaining fill as an island in the centre. At the bottom a wattle lining *c*.1.1m in diameter was uncovered, similar in form to that recorded in all the other wells examined. Unfortunately the lining rapidly collapsed, but a sample of the wattles and sails all proved to be alder. The upper fills of the well shaft consisted of silty clay loam containing some rubbish deposition, though not in abundance, suggesting that there were not large quantities of demolition material to be disposed of when it was filled. The waterlogged lower fill indicated two main types of local habitat, grassland and wetland, and suggested that the material had accumulated naturally.

This continued activity on the fort site presupposes that the area remained enclosed. There is no direct evidence of refurbishment of the rampart, but since the workshop was recessed into it, it is likely to have remained upstanding as long as that building was in use. Moreover, the east and west gates were clearly remodelled. The refurbishment of the east gate was evidenced by the laying of a cobble base around the curve of the inturned rampart over the original road surface (*74*). The cobbling consisted of a single layer of angular, mainly waterworn cobbles of varying sizes up to some 0.3m across. It was best preserved on the south side of the gate where it was as much as 2.5m wide, the outer edge defined by a kerb made up of some of the larger stones. The rampart may have been cut back slightly, for the cobbles extended around two sides of one of the outer post pits of the south tower. Though the cobbling did not survive well immediately outside the gate portal, sufficient of the alignment of the kerb remained inside it to indicate that the rampart had extended across the south portal effectively blocking it. The cobbling on the north side of the gate passage was more fragmentary, surviving only in patches. However, a probable outer kerb line of larger stones indicated a maximum width of 3.0m for the rampart extension. This widening of the rampart narrowed the road leading to the gateway to 3.0m and funnelled traffic towards the north portal.

The history of the west gate was more complex. It was apparently decommissioned a second time, for a V-shaped ditch up to 2.9m wide and 1.5m deep was dug across the entrance passage and through the road metalling (see *71*), clipping four of the six secondary post pits that defined the entrance passage. Presumably this involved the dismantling of the gateway at the same time, though the only direct evidence of this comes from two secondary post pits in the south tower where the posts had clearly been removed. This decommissioning was probably, therefore, contemporary with the dismantling of the buildings in the interior, though this cannot positively be demonstrated. But the blocking ditch was in use for only a relatively brief period, with a maximum of 0.25m of natural silting containing some charcoal lenses accumulating at the bottom, before it was deliberately packed with sandy clay largely devoid of finds (*colour plate 25*) and was sealed by a re-facing of the rampart on the south side of the entrance passage. This was evidenced by the laying of a cobble base some 2.5m wide around the curve of the rampart (see *71*) overlying the primary road surface. The cobbling consisted of the fragmentary remains of a single layer of both angular and waterworn cobbles of varying sizes up to 0.35m across, the outer edge defined by a kerb made up of some of the larger and more angular stones. The kerb could be traced only as far as the midpoint of the infilled ditch, but similar cobbling extended into the interior of the fort, overlying the intervallum road, the *via principalis* and the north-west corner of barrack 12. This serves to link the re-facing of the rampart here to the cobbling over of the fort interior after the buildings had been demolished.

Towards the end of its working life, probably after the demolition of the buildings within the fort, the annexe was subdivided by a substantial ditch (801 and 120) some 4.0-4.5m wide and 0.8-1.1m deep running in a straight line parallel to, and some 55m from, the western defences of the fort and situated immediately to the west of an earlier dividing gully. It stopped short of the outer annexe ditch to both north and south and also butt ended on either side of the main road from the west gate of the fort, widening to some 5.7m over the last 2.5m of its length to frame an entrance. A second shallow

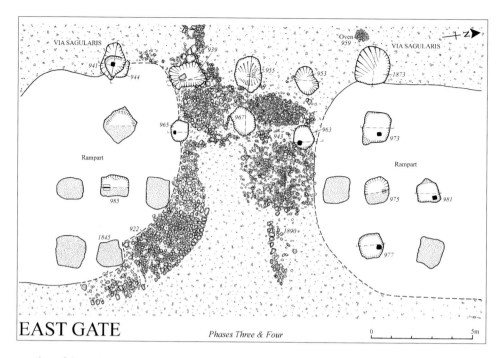

74 Plan of the east gate: phase 3 & 4

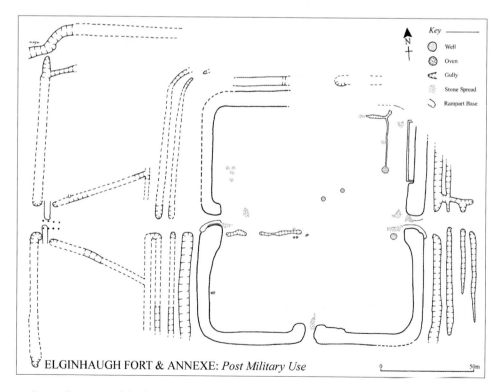

75 Post-military use of the fort enclosure and annexe

ditch 2.0-3.0m wide with a broad U-shaped profile abutted it almost at right angles some 8m from its northern end in trench 5 (see *35*), running broadly parallel with, and some 19m inside, the primary northern ditch of the annexe. Unfortunately, this ditch was not detected in trench 6, so that its limits remain undefined. However, assuming it to have been continuous as far as the outer ditches of the fort, the combined effect of these two ditches was to demarcate an area of slightly more than 0.8ha (2 acres) within the annexe immediately adjacent to the fort. At the same time the annexe was further subdivided into three elements by two ditches, one on either side of and running at an acute angle to the road. They were consistently V-shaped, but with a more gently sloping side facing the road and varying in width from 2.7m to 3.2m and in depth from 0.8m to 1.1m. At their western ends, they abutted the rear of the new gate (below), while at their eastern ends they were linked into the outer fort ditches, which had already heavily silted up by this time. These ditches formed a funnel between the outer fort ditch and the entrance to the inner part of the annexe (*75*).

The main ditch dividing the annexe presumably had an associated bank or rampart, though the only traces which survived were in trench 1 by the entrance. Here the rampart, which was of turf some 3m wide, ran approximately 2m behind the dividing ditch, though the inturned ends of the ditch brought the rampart to its lip. Indeed, much of the superstructure had later collapsed, or more likely been pushed, into the ends of the dividing ditch and also into the ends of the funnel ditches which encroached to within just over a metre of the back of the rampart.

The rampart abutted the front third of a simple single-portal gateway constructed on eight relatively small post holes spaced at regular intervals of 2.8m (*76* and *colour plate 26*). The width of the portal varied between 3.1m and 3.8m, as measured between the inside edges of post impressions, which were recorded in four of the post holes. Seven of the eight posts were revealed and sectioned, but there was no time at the end of the excavation to investigate the presumed eighth which lay outside trench 1. Though the surviving post impressions indicated posts equal to, or even larger than, those employed in the fort gates, the implication of the relatively shallow depth of the post holes, which average only just over half that of the fort gates, is that the superstructure is unlikely to have risen above the level of the first storey. A height of approximately 3m is assumed, as for the fort gates, to allow sufficient clearance for loaded wagons or mounted riders. Any linkage at that level from one side of the gate to the other is more likely to have been designed to ensure the stability of the structure and prevent inward collapse of the sides than to facilitate access across the top of the gate. Direct analogies for this form of the gateway are extremely difficult to find. The closest, though built on only six posts, is the south gate of the Flavian fort at Fendoch, which opens into an annexe.

Immediately outside this gate, along the north side of the road, a construction slot and series of post holes indicated the presence of a fence or similar barrier preventing immediate access to this side of the outer annexe (*76*). A discontinuous rough cobble spread extended the area of hardstanding 4-5m south from the edge of the road and around the butt end of the dividing ditch. Similar, but much less extensive areas of cobbling were evident just inside the gate in trench 1 and in the north-west corner of trench 3.

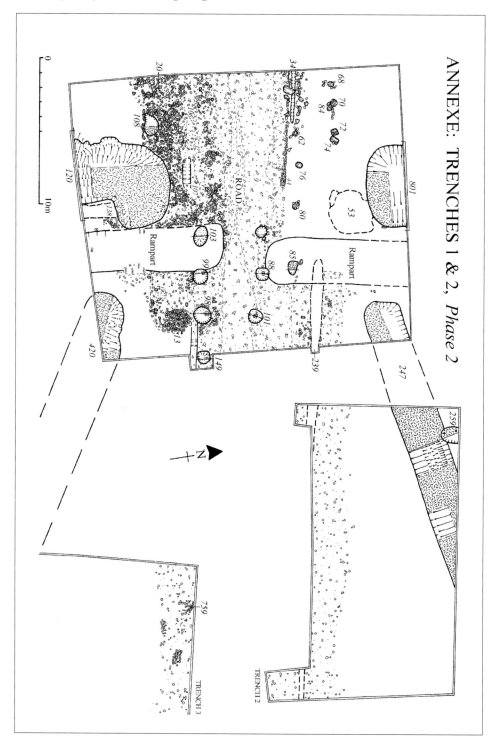

ANNEXE: TRENCHES 1 & 2, *Phase 2*

76 Plan of annexe trenches 1 and 2, phase 2: gateway

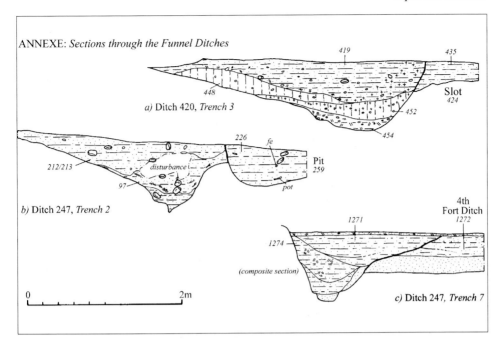

ANNEXE: *Sections through the Funnel Ditches*

a) Ditch 420, Trench 3

b) Ditch 247, Trench 2

c) Ditch 247, Trench 7

77 Sections through the funnel ditches across the annexe

The subdivision of annexes is not commonly attested, though aerial photographs of the broadly contemporary forts at Easter Happrew and Dalswinton show ditches cutting across the annexes there. The arrangement of the funnel ditches, however, is entirely without parallel in a military context. Nonetheless, their location, layout and profile are all consistent in the particular function that they indicate. They were clearly designed to channel movement, presumably of animals, from the west gate of the fort along the road and out through the single portal annexe gateway into the outer part of the annexe without entering the inner part (75). The gentle inner slope of the ditch would have reduced the possibility of broken limbs if the animals strayed off the road, while the steep outer face would have ensured than they could not get away (77). Nor was there any avenue of escape at either end, for the ditches ran into the outer ditch of the fort to the east and abutted the back of the annexe rampart to the west. On a domestic site of later prehistoric date such a configuration of ditches would almost certainly be assumed to relate to the control of stock movement, such as the antennae ditches at Gussage all Saints and Little Woodbury. Indeed, such an interpretation ties in very well with the provision of improved hardstanding within the fort enclosure; the additional water supply provided by the three new wells, and the greater proportion of barley and oats, more usually employed for feeding animals than troops, recorded in the post-fort occupation deposits from one of the ovens and one of the wells.

The context for this activity is less easily determined and not readily paralleled. It might at first be thought that it represents the takeover of the enclosure by the native population for agricultural purposes. But the character of the remains, particularly the gateways, the field ovens and the wells, is so clearly Roman that the continued involvement of the military must be presumed. Evidence of human occupation within the enclosure is very limited, restricted to a few cooking ovens, so its most likely function would appear to be as a collecting point for animals. We know that on occasions Roman troops foraged widely for supplies, including animals for both food and transport. An undated waxed tablet from a native settlement at Tolsum north of the Rhine in Friesland records the purchase, by what appears to be a military buyer, of a cow from a civilian, while according to Tacitus traders were wandering all over that area in AD 69. One of the writing tablets from Vindolanda of early second-century date, a letter from Octavius to Candidus, refers to trading activity involving cereals, sinew and hides. The quantities and sums involved strongly suggest that the individuals concerned were involved in military supply. There is also evidence that taxation, particularly in frontier areas, could be assessed in kind. Indeed, it has recently been argued by David Braund that this may have been the rule rather than the exception. Most apposite here is the treatment of the Frisii, a tribe who lived on the north side of the Rhine beyond the area occupied by Roman troops in what is now the Netherlands. According to Tacitus, after their submission to Drusus in 12 BC, he imposed tribute on them in the form of ox hides for military use. A collection centre is precisely the sort of facility that would have been useful for such a regular and systematised process as tax collection. What is particularly interesting is that such a centre was maintained at Elginhaugh in an area only recently abandoned by the Roman army. This adds considerably to the otherwise scattered and fragmentary evidence of direct control extending beyond territory formally garrisoned by Roman troops. It also lends further support to the theory that the local tribe, the Votadini, like the Frisii, may have been in some form of treaty relationship with Rome, if they continued to pay tribute after the withdrawal of a formal garrison from the area.

How long this arrangement continued in force cannot readily be established. On historical grounds it is unlikely to have continued beyond the second stage of withdrawal from Scotland in the early years of the second century AD (above, chapter two). There are, however, no associated artefacts which might suggest that the activity continued for any lengthy period and so it may have lasted no more than a year or two. There are slight indications that when this secondary use of the annexe did come to an end, the defences were deliberately slighted. The butt ends of the funnel ditches were full of turf, as if the rampart had been pushed into them; a rubbish or demolition pit cut the more northerly funnel ditch in trench 2, and the post holes of the annexe gate in trench 1 showed some signs of disturbance. However, this process of deliberate demolition may have been only partial, since elsewhere the annexe ditches appear to have silted up naturally. The Romans never returned to the site at Elginhaugh. When they resumed their occupation of Scotland in the mid-second century AD under the emperor Antoninus Pius, the focus of military occupation was moved some 5km further north to the mouth of the River Esk at Inveresk by Musselburgh.

FURTHER READING

It has been decided not to encumber the text with the full reference system normally employed in academic publications, so as not to break up the flow of the text and make it less off-putting for the general reader. Similarly, recommendations for further reading are restricted to books, which are likely to be more accessible to most readers, either in bookshops or larger libraries, rather than articles in sometimes obscure scholarly journals or collections of papers. Those who wish to pursue particular points or seek fuller detail of the site at Elginhaugh itself should turn to the full excavation report, which is provided with detailed academic references, published by the Roman Society in the Britannia Monograph series (William S. Hanson 2007 *Elginhaugh: a Flavian fort and its annexe*).

Though there are a number of books, including some quite recent ones, which address the Roman conquest of Scotland in the first century, they are of variable quality and reliability. My own *Agricola and the conquest of the north* (2nd ed. Batsford 1991), now sadly out of print, offers a fairly comprehensive analysis of the period which is still valid though inevitably out of date in relation to the results of excavations over the last fifteen years. David Breeze's *Roman Scotland* (Historic Scotland/Batsford (2nd ed. 2006), is more up-to-date, but adopts a wider chronological canvas and takes a more thematical approach. The recent volume by David Woolliscroft and Birgitta Hoffman *Rome's first frontier: The Flavian occupation of northern Scotland* (Tempus 2006) provides much valuable and fully up-to-date information about Roman remains of first-century date north of the Forth-Clyde isthmus, but its conclusions about the minimal role of Agricola in the conquest of Scotland should be treated with caution, for the reasons I make clear in chapter two.

The best general book on Roman forts is still Anne Johnson's *Roman forts* (A.C. Black 1983), though Paul Bidwell's *Roman forts in Britain* (Batsford/English Heritage 1997) provides a more recent and very useful overview of the British evidence. Books are not available on all aspects of military building, but two volumes in the British Archaeological Reports series, by Michael J. Jones (*Roman fort defences to AD 117*. BAR British Series 21, 1975) and David P. Davison (*The barracks of the Roman army from the first to the third centuries A.D.* BAR International Series 472, 1989) provide valuable detailed studies of those topics.

Useful parallels with the site at Elginhaugh can be obtained by consulting other excavations reports. Important contemporary examples from Scotland include Shepherd S. Frere and John J. Wilkes *Strageath: excavations within the Roman fort, 1973-86* (Britannia Monograph Series 9, 1989) and Lynn Pitts and J.K.S. St Joseph *Inchtuthil: the Roman legionary fortress* (Britannia Monograph Series 6, 1985), while Michael R. McCarthy's *Roman Carlisle and the lands of the Solway* (Tempus 2002) provides a general summary of the importance evidence from Carlisle in advance of its full publication. Nick Hodgson's *The Roman fort at Wallsend (Segedunum): Excavations in 1997-98* (Tyne and Wear Museums Archaeological Monograph 2, 2003) is of particular importance for its identification of stable barracks.

Books on the Roman army are legion. Specifically related to Britain is Paul A. Holder's *The Roman army in Britain* (Batsford 1982). Of particular relevance to understanding the development of the debate about cavalry accommodation and stables is *The Roman cavalry* by Karen R. Dixon and Pat Southern (Batsford 1992), while Mike C. Bishop and Jon C.N. Coulston have written the standard text on *Roman military equipment from the Punic Wars to the Fall of Rome* (2nd ed. Oxbow 2006) and Michel Feugère provides a very useful overview of the *Weapons of the Romans* (Tempus 2002). Different aspects of the nature of life in the Roman army are covered in a very useful volume of collected papers by Roy W. Davies, edited by David Breeze and Valerie Maxfield (*Service in the Roman army*. Edinburgh University Press 1989), while Alan Bowman provides an excellent popular account of some of the Vindolanda ink tablets in his *Life and letters on the Roman frontier: Vindolanda and its people* (British Museum Press 1994). Overviews of various aspects of the material evidence from Roman sites, though not confined to the military, can be found in a new book *The Artefacts of Roman Britain: their purpose and use*, edited by Lindsay Allason-Jones (Cambridge University Press forthcoming).

There is no general work which covers fort annexes, though Sebastian Sommer's *The military vici in Roman Britain: aspects of their origins, their location and layout, administration, function and end* (BAR British Series 129, 1984) considers the evidence for civil settlements and argues the case for annexes being so interpreted.

The nature of Iron Age society and the impact of the Roman presence on the indigenous population generally is usefully considered in a volume of collected papers edited by Kevin J. Edwards and Ian B.M. Ralston (*Scotland after the ice age: environment, archaeology and history, 8000 BC - 1000 AD*. Edinburgh University Press 2003) and by Dennis W. Harding in his *The Iron Age in Northern Britain: Celts and Romans, Natives and Invaders* (Routledge 2004) which, though recently published, is less fully up-to-date on issues of Romanisation. Detailed consideration of the relevant environmental evidence is provided by Marike van der Veen in her *Crop husbandry regimes: an archaeobotanical study of farming in northern England 1000BC-AD500* (Sheffield University 1992), while the full report on the important nearby excavations at Port Seton by Colin Haselgrove and Rod McCullagh is available as a monograph (*An Iron Age coastal community in East Lothian: the excavation of two later prehistoric enclosure complexes at Fishers Road, Port Seton, 1994-5*. STAR Monograph 6, Edinburgh 2000).

INDEX

Figure and colour plate numbers are in brackets after main entries

Gates
    annexe 149, 151, 152 (*77, colour plate 26*)
    fort 32-3, 42, 44, 46, 48, 50-2, 62-4, 66, 84-5,
    106, 130-1, 132, 147 (*9, 10, 16, 52, 66, 71, 74,
    colour plates 8, 9, 15, 16, 25*)
Geophysical survey 87, 99, 114
Germany 19, 26, 31, 50, 70, 72, 102, 123, 124
Glass
    beads 75
    gaming pieces 128
    general 22, 24-5, 31-2, 35, 134
    recycling 114
    vessels 119, 124-5, 126, 132, 133 (*60*)
Glenlochar, fort 12
Graffito 124
Grain *see* cereals
Granaries 28, 42, 43-4, 46, 50, 57-8, 65, 117, 124,
    141, 143, 145 (*21, colour plates 11, 20*)

Haltern, fortress 50
Hayton, fort 26, 87
Headquarters building 28, 30-1, 35, 41, 42, 43,
    53-7, 65, 75, 108, 110, 116, 117, 126, 131, 134,
    137 (*8, 18, 19, 53, colour plates 13, 18*)
Hearths 56, 70-2, 94, 107-8, 110 (*53*)
Hipposandal 106
Historic Scotland 14, 15, 17
Hoard *see* coins
Hobley, Andrew 34
Hodgson, Nick 72, 79, 81
Hoffman, Birgitta 25
Horse harness 73, 75, 101 (*32*)
Horses
    feeding/watering 69, 72, 126, 140-1
    general 26, 60, 75, 99, 106, 118
    stabling 61, 68, 70, 72-3, 75, 78-81, 105, 130,
    135
Hyginus 68, 79
Hypocaust 127

Inchtuthil, fortress 12, 28, 31, 34, 35, 37, 45, 75, 77,
    78, 98, 110, 116, 122, 130
Industrial activity 87, 94, 98-100, 106-110
Infantry 41, 67-8, 70, 73, 78, 78, 81, 122, 124
Inkwells 114
Inveresk, fort 139, 152
Inverquharity, fort 12
Iron Age 11, 15, 137, 138-9, 140, 141
Iron
    equipment 101, 105-6, 114, 124, 132 (*45, 46,
    51, 54*)
    nails 35, 44
    working 60, 93-4, 106, 110, 143 (*41*)

Johnson, Anne 87
Justinian 41

Kilns 89, 91, 93, 94, 99, 112, 114
King, Tony 140
Kintore camp 26, 144

Ladenburg, civil settlement 72
Ladyward, fort 67
Latrines 57, 117, 119, 127, 128-30, 135 (*65, colour
    plate 19*)
Leather 104 (*48-9*)
Legio II Adiutrix 37
Legio XXth Valeria Victrix 37
Legionaries 26, 27, 29, 36, 37, 41, 62, 68, 77-8,
    101, 127 (*24*)
Longthorpe, fortress 94
Lorica segmentata *see* armour
Lunt, Baginton, fort 46, 58, 63 (*colour plates 15,
    20*)
Lyon ware *see* pottery

Maintenance 65-6, 105-6
Malling, fort 12, 87
Manufacture, local 31, 60, 100, 106-8, 112-4
Maxwell, Gordon 11, 12, 127, 137
Medical instruments 132 (*68*)
Melville Nurseries, camp 144
Mesolithic 137
Metalworking *see* iron and copper alloy
Milton, fort 87, 100
Minerva 135
Mollins, fort 12, 22, 87 (*colour plate 4*)
Monktonhall, camp 144
Mons Graupius 26
Mortaria *see* pottery
Mumrills, fort 85

Nails *see* iron
Needle 105-6 (*51*)
Neolithic 11, 137
Nero, emperor 21, 29, 31, 32
Netherlands 117, 142, 152
Newstead, fort 13, 24, 37, 39, 78, 79, 87, 94, 98,
    99-100, 111, 116, 127
North Esk (river) 12, 14, 28, 48, 127, 137

Oakwood, fort 87
Oats *see* cereals
Oberstimm, fort 98
Old Kilpatrick, fort 85
Olive oil 119, 133, 141
Opus signinum 127